FACETS
OF LIBERTY:

A Libertarian Primer

Edited by
L.K. Samuels

With assistance from Elizabeth Brierly
And Jane Heider

FREELAND PRESS and Rampart Institute

First Edition, 1985
Second Edition, revised, 2009

L.K. Samuels
Facets of Liberty: A Libertarian Primer
ISBN 978-0-578-00310-8
1. Politics   2. Libertarianism   3. Philosophy
I. Title   II. Samuels, L.K.

Dedicated to:

William F. Heider

1914-2004

CONTENTS

1985 FOREWORD

The intellectual libertarian movement rivals the birth of Christ in its significance in human affairs.

No doubt this comparison is an exaggeration, but I do believe that time will show the extreme importance of libertarianism to our descendents throughout future centuries. I feel that generations will look back to this period and marvel at the early libertarian writers and activists. They will wonder how these early libertarians ever conceived such self–evident notions of voluntarism and non–coercion. They will be astonished at how anyone could survive the daily barrage of statism—regulation, taxation, and aggression.

With this in mind, I decided to gather some of the better libertarian material to preserve for all time. I was afraid that many of these important articles would be lost in dusty garages or dark archives. The reason I say this is that so many of these articles had limited circulation; they were published in now–defunct magazines and newsletters. In some ways, I feel that I am archiving this material for future archivists.

Facets of Liberty: A Libertarian Primer has been published to give a general, overall view of the libertarian philosophy. It is meant primarily for beginners. However, it was a challenge to find articles that deal in simple libertarian basics. Some of the essays reach beyond the simple and the general, but I have arranged the chapters in an order that I hope will give beginners a chance to understand the ideas, right from the start.

–L. K. Samuels, Editor

2009 FOREWORD

I still remember the first time someone called me a libertarian. It was September 1968. I was 17 years old and my eyes were still wide from having read almost everything Ayn Rand had written. I had started arguing with some of my professors at the University of Winnipeg, where I was an undergrad. That particular day, I was proselytizing a left-wing sociology professor named Katherine George. Frustrated that she could not persuade me, she said, "You sound like one of those libertarians."

"Those what?" I said, mystified.

"Those libertarians," she answered.

"What's a libertarian?" I asked, mentally picturing a naked librarian.

"You know," she said, "those people who ran the student newspaper last year. Clancy Smith. Dennis Owens."

"No," I answered, "but thank you for telling me. I'll look them up."

"S**t," she said.

Little did I know that day that I was part of a fledgling movement, a movement that would grow in Canada, where I lived, in the United States, the mother church of libertarianism, and in many other countries.

The change has been dramatic. Libertarians are no longer impotent gadflies. Now we are potent gadflies. We have become serious players in the national and international arena. Since the beginning of the 21st century, libertarians have flexed their newly acquired muscles, and libertarianism is now acknowledged as a revival of the "classical liberalism" that had challenged monarchs and tyrants during the Enlightenment. We have new tyrants to challenge, and they are not in scarce supply.

When I began to think of myself as a libertarian, days after Professor George called me one, I could, in a few hours a day, read almost every libertarian publication. Forty years later, although I read much faster, I couldn't read every libertarian publication even if I spent sixty hours a week reading them. And although it's not hard to find current libertarian articles on line, it's harder to find articles from the late 1960s. And, as in all areas of life, 90 percent of everything you find is low-quality or mediocre.

That's where Facets of Liberty comes in. These are the classics of liberty from the late 1960s, and all of them are good. Except for the additional material added in this second edition, most of the articles are from the libertarian student era that exploded on the scene at the University of California at Berkeley in the mid-1960s. Across the nation, hundreds of libertarian organizations and underground newspapers began to dot the landscape. One in particular was Society for a Libertarian Life (SLL). Lawrence Samuels, a commercial art student at California State University, Fullerton, founded SLL in 1973. SLL published its own campus journal and issue papers. Lawrence has compiled these articles, which represent the seasoned judgment of a man who has been a lover of liberty for more than a third of a century. Enjoy.

--David R. Henderson

CHAPTER 1

WHO AUTHORIZES THE AUTHORITIES?

By Butler D. Shaffer

I began my class one day with an apparently simple question: "Does the U.S. Constitution have legitimacy?" As a follow–up question, I asked, "By what right did one group of men get together and impose upon others a particular system of government?"

These questions, of course, do not apply only to the American political system, but can be asked, with equal force, of every government that has ever existed. By what right did the Bolsheviks, or the Catholic Church, or William the Conqueror, or Genghis Khan, or any other group or individual, assume the authority to make and enforce laws upon other men and women?

Having been educated in traditional schools, most of my students answered with the kind of conditioned responses that it has been the purpose of traditional education to provide.

"We all got together and agreed to this form of government," they declared.

Even though the fallacy of such explanations of governmental origins were quickly dispelled by asking the students to tell me the place and date at which they attended this "meeting" with "everybody else" to establish a government, I have no doubt that all of them truly believed that the American government was formed out of the common consent of all Americans.

I forged ahead with my questions: "If we all have inalienable rights, how can some men vote to take away the rights of others?"   "How does the fact that ten men may choose to join together for their common protection, impose upon the eleventh man any obligation to go along with them?"

True to their public school upbringings, my students tried to take comfort in the processes of voting: "If the majority is in favor of something, that makes it right," a number of them agreed.

"But what makes the will of the majority sacrosanct?" I asked.

I went on. "Suppose three muggers confront you on the street and say, 'We want your money. But don't worry—we're going to let you vote on whether or not you should give it to us.' If this group votes three–to–one in favor of taking your money, does this legitimize its actions?"

A few of my students saw the obvious analogy to government, but for others, the characterization of government as nothing more than sanctified theft and violence was too unsettling. One student tried to rehabilitate the democratic process with the weak plea that "it has to involve more than just a few people," while another felt obliged to defend democracy and voting at all costs, as something in the nature of an ultimate principle. "Majority rule is just the way our government is set up," he argued, not seeing that he had succeeded in arguing himself into one big circle.

"But that's what I am asking you to explain." I went on: "How does this—or any other—system of government acquire the legitimacy to impose such processes upon those who do not choose to be bound by it?"   The discussion ended with a number of my students resorting to the traditional method of all totalitarian systems and ideas: "If you don't like it, you should leave the country," they shouted.

When the discussion was over, one of my students stated that this had been a very "unsettling" and "uncomfortable" experience.

"It was my purpose to make you uncomfortable," I replied, "for only in facing hard, uncomfortable questions will we be able to overcome the dependencies on authority that we have accepted for our lives."   I remarked upon how institutions not only cause most of the social conflict in the world today, but absolutely require conflict in order to maintain their power over our lives. Government, in particular, generates and manages conflict, and in the process, solidifies its base of power over us.

"But what's the answer to this?" a number of them asked. "What alternatives are there for us?" I told them that since the problem of government involves our self–induced dependencies upon authority figures, for me to give you my answer is simply to substitute me as your new authority.

The social problems in our world are occasioned by our consciousness. They are the product of how we think— about ourselves, others, and our responsibilities for our own behavior and our own conclusions. "The answer," I concluded, "is that you must figure out your own answers."

That has always been the source of the human dilemma. Because we have come to enjoy the luxury of having other people make judgments and decisions for us, we are terribly uncomfortable when someone comes along and challenges our complacency.

We enjoy triviality—a fact that has spawned mindless television programming, gossip magazines, and a general banality in what used to be the art of serious conversation—and eschew fundamental inquiries. But if life is to have any meaning, and if we are ever to overcome the viciousness and vulgarity that are destroying the quality of human life, we must get ourselves into the habit of asking the sorts of questions we have been trained not to ask.

A prolific writer and speaker, Butler D. Shaffer has been Professor of Law at Southwestern School of Law in Los Angeles since 1977, and he has taught law and economics at LeFevre's Rampart College in Colorado. He is author of *Calculated Chaos: Institutional Threats to Peace and Human Survival* (1985), *In the Restraint of Trade* (1997), and *The Wizards of Ozymandias* (2002). He is a frequent contributor to LewRockwell.com. This essay was first published in *The Orange County Register* in the 1980's.

CHAPTER 2

VOLUNTARISM: THE ABSENCE OF FORCE

By L.K. Samuels

...the State calls its own violence law, and that of the individual, crime.

–Max Stirner

Voluntarism, as a philosophy advocating the absence of aggression, underlies every important issue of the day. Every issue has two directions from which it may be approached: (1) individuals may attempt to solve problems by voluntary interaction among people, or (2) individuals may attempt to solve problems by involuntary interaction among people. The difference is that the latter implements force.

The best way to show the striking contrast between voluntarism and force is to give an explicit example. One of the worst crimes is to assault another human being, especially by rape. When someone is sexually assaulted, a coercive action has been perpetrated against the body and liberty of another person. No consent has been given to the rapist, therefore, the victim's right not to be physically aggressed upon is violated. That is to say, the victim is forced by the physical strength of the attacker. The victim is robbed of his or her freedom, and made a slave of the attacker until the attacker either leaves the victim or the victim submits to the attacker's wishes.

When a person consents freely to engage in sex, no crime has been committed, as there is no victim. In what is commonly called prostitution, a woman gives her consent to her customer—otherwise it is rape. Brute force characterizes the one; peaceful consent, the other.

VOLUNTARISM

Voluntarism holds simply that people should be at liberty to choose their own lifestyles without being forced to follow someone else's. Followers of voluntarism (i.e., voluntarists) believe that people cannot be forced to be good or perfect, and that no authority has any business trying through the use or threat of violence to protect people from themselves.

Voluntarism opposes any compulsory or mandatory program, no matter what reasons or justifications are cited. It is true, for instance, that slums need to be cleared, the unemployed need jobs, and the poor need money. However, at whose expense are these wrongs to be righted? Should society or government, in the name of the slum dwellers, the unemployed, or the poor, rob those who were industrious, enterprising, or fortunate enough to gather some wealth? And by the way, who would decide whose wealth is to be confiscated, and how much of it?

Should slum dwellers be physically dragged from their rooms to make way for urban renewal? Should apartment owners have their land forcibly seized under the power of eminent domain? If so, who would decide whose land is to be condemned?

Certainly, problems of the community and the individual need to be resolved, but must we resort to threats of jail and violence to control people and situations? When physical control of each person by government is accepted and practiced, where will this ultimately lead? How far can aggression and force go before they are declared to be out of hand? It should be realized and understood that if government has the authority to give what everybody wants, then it has the authority to take what everybody has.

AGGRESSION

The opposite of voluntarism is aggression. Aggression is an unprovoked and unjustified assault or invasion upon peaceful individuals (or their property), who pose no physical threat to the attacker. For example, there is nothing inherently moral or immoral concerning transportation of people by bus. Yet, when people are compelled by fear of arrest or jail for refusing to comply with forced busing programs, aggression against the parents has been committed. The parents have lost their right of consent. They have been abused. What was their so–called crime? They refused to comply. But they have committed no acts of violence against anyone.

Again, persons of authoritarian persuasion abandon voluntary approaches to problems, because such approaches often fail to accomplish what the authoritarian believes ought to be accomplished. The authoritarian believes that if someone fails to follow along, then, by George, that person must suffer the consequences. After all, they believe, it is for the good of society. Society is perceived as a grand institution based on foundations of granite. In actuality, there is no physical structure known as "society." Society is not physical; it cannot be touched with a finger. Society is a mere concept; individuals are real. The authoritarian whose arguments rely on the concept of taking action for the "good of society" is usually the one who benefits the most from society's social and bureaucratic programs.

The main trouble with aggression is that it can never be limited. It is commonly believed that a little force, if limited, is acceptable. But what is the limit? And who sets it? How far can taxation go? Can government take 90% of a worker's income? It has the authority. Only certain circumstances prevent a particular government from going too far. In the case of Hitler's and Stalin's government, indeed, it went too far. To paraphrase Prof. Murray Rothbard, once you justify the existence of aggression, once you sanction the use of force to control people, for no matter what reason, you can justify every other evil and excess of the state.

After one form of aggression is legislated or dictated, what prevents the enactment of another? For example, if it is permissible to draft men into the military, why not draft teachers into schools, and workers into factories? Where is the limit? In fact, during World War II, a number of U.S. politicians introduced federal legislation to draft workers into war–related industries. Why not? they reasoned. After all, Hitler was doing it.

NATURAL LAW VIOLATED

Aggression is a direct violation of the nature of men and women. When controls are applied, a person is compelled to act contrary to his conscience; otherwise, force would not have been necessary.

If, for instance, a person wishes to hitchhike, and is willing to take the associated risks, that person should be able to enjoy that liberty, since no physical aggression is involved. But when a government body enacts a law prohibiting hitchhiking, then a proponent of that activity is forced to act contrary to his convictions. He knows that hitchhiking infringes on no one's rights, but if he follows his desires and convictions, he is faced with possibly fines or even imprisonment.

Such victimless crime laws attack the very nature of a person's reliance upon reason. That is, since men and women are capable of rational thinking, and since survival depends on remaining loyal to one's peaceful judgments, utilizing physical force to direct their actions is to place them in situations in which they must act contrary to their rational nature. Instead of following their own convictions, they are compelled to follow the legislated or dictated convictions of rulers; and since many laws are political, having little to do with rationality or reality, people are forced to follow corrupt and inept laws, and to deny their own self–interest.

At this point, survival becomes a matter of obeying governmental edicts. In such a controlled society, the individual is made to be responsive to politics and politicians. Personal convictions are manipulated for the sake of political expediency.

This situation causes people to look toward government instead of to themselves for decisions on morality and ethics. Authority becomes all–important, and citizens are led to believe that without a controlling, decision–making authority and its guidance, civilization would cease to function. In fact, what will cease to function is the individual's independence, self–esteem, and reliance upon logic.

FREEDOM AND GOVERNMENT

History shows that men always attempt to control other men. One of the best methods to control others is to organize a select few into a gang. The gang receives further support by announcing its intention to prevent other gangs from doing what the first gang already does. People are led to believe that with one big gang, crime will be minimized, since crimes by local, small–time crooks will be prohibited. But who protects the citizen from the big gang? Who polices the police? Who inspects the inspectors? Who oversees the overseers?

A popular cartoon strip provided insight into this matter. It depicted a professor explaining to his students, "Our government will establish laws to protect the individual's right to privacy."

"Who will enforce them?" one student asked.

The professor answered calmly, "The C.I.A."

Government can no more protect freedom than a burglar can protect a bank. To be blunt, the governments of the world make Billy the Kid and Jesse James look like lovable characters in a Mother Goose bedtime story. Nobody—from the crooks in government to the gangsters lurking on the street corner—should have at their disposal the authority to use force.

Freedom is the absence of aggression, and government is the absence of voluntarism. The two—freedom and government—cannot coexist for long. Sooner or later, one must consume the other. The trouble is, liberty always seems to be the first one devoured.

The absence of aggression and violence in government prevents crooks from using the authority of government to promote their self–interest. No one can manipulate other people's lives without the power of physical violence. But governments themselves have a monopoly on force. Until voluntarism is given more chances, politics will continue as usual, and freedom will be another flickering candle in the wind.

The manager and co–manager of the Future of Freedom Conference series for five years in the 1980's, L.K. Samuels is a writer and libertarian activist. He founded Society for Libertarian Life (SLL) at the California State University, Fullerton in the early 1970's. He was instrumental in forming Rampart Institute, based on the works of Robert LeFevre. Former Northern Vice Chair of the Libertarian Party of California (2003-2007), he has authored a series of fiction and nonfiction books. Web site: www.Freedom1776.com. This article was published in the 1970s as a position paper for SLL.

CHAPTER 3

A BETTER WORLD: AN ALLEGORY

By Douglas Casey

Out beyond the blue horizon, but somewhere under the rainbow, lay the island continent of Minerva. It was divided into a number of regions, but by far the most pleasing was composed of the countries of Anarchia and Dystopia, known collectively as Anartopia. They were, until a set of rather odd ideas took hold in Dystopia, identical in most respects, and a person could tell which region he was in only by noting whether he was on the east or the west side of the mountain range that divided them.

Although the people on Minerva differed from those elsewhere only in some of the ideas they held, their lifestyle varied considerably. Visitors were amazed to find that not only did the telephones work, but everyone had one. The water was safe to drink; the toilets flushed; and the trains ran on time. It was a happy land, where children could remember their grandmothers in checked aprons baking pies and bread in the ovens of their snug homes. Some visitors made jokes about how it was all rather like a Norman Rockwell painting, or perhaps a television commercial for a "natural" breakfast cereal.

Each person did what he found he could do best, and exchanged his services daily with others in the marketplace. Some wrote books; others grew corn, or made cars, or pumped oil, or tailored suits; and still others made sure that these things were transported from one place to another. In any event, everyone was able to do exactly as he pleased, as long as he did not physically harm his neighbor or his neighbor's property. It was because of that, and the fact that everyone could do what he liked with his own property, that the land was to everyone's liking. Of course, not everyone owned land (and some residents were far wealthier than others), but someone who wanted something had only to trade its present owner a good or service that he valued more highly when the exchange was made; it was assumed both men thought they were better off. As each man produced what he was most efficiently able to, and exchanged it with others, the wealth of the region grew, and everyone was, indeed, better off.

Life was stable and pleasant, but not because of any altruism on the part of the residents. Each man produced only because it was to his best advantage to do so. The baker baked bread not because he wanted to keep the others from starving, but because he wanted the good things the others would trade him for it. Rather than barter with one another for their respective products, however, the Anartopians, being sophisticated in financial matters, used a medium of exchange. Over the years—over thousands of years, in fact—a certain yellow metal had proved very suited to this purpose. Just as both theory and practice had taught that bricks were good for building houses, uranium good for use as nuclear fuel, and paper good for printing books, gold proved uniquely suited for use as money. Perhaps in the past, people had tried using uranium for houses, or gold for nuclear fuel, or paper for money—but no one was very interested in the results.

Just as warehouses grew up, out of convenience, for storage of such things as grain, other warehouses grew up for the storage of gold. Instead of carrying the heavy metal with him on a shopping trip, an Anartopian needed only to carry warehouse receipts representing gold he had in storage. People would accept these paper receipts in trade for their produce, if they were sure both that the other party had gold there himself, and that his warehouse—also called a "bank"—would pay on demand. Only a fool would confuse the paper receipt with the money it represented, any more than he could confuse a grain receipt with the grain it represented.

All the banks were all run by entrepreneurs for a profit, not as a public service; they made a profit, however, only because they provided a public service. People generally deposited their gold only in those banks deemed most conservative and worthy of trust; accordingly, all the banks competed with one another in conservatism and trustworthiness, because that was the profitable thing to do.

People chose their insurance companies on the same basis. It was possible to buy a policy covering practically any financial or personal loss that had a monetary value, and being prudent (and money–oriented), the Anartopians generally took advantage of the policies. There were even policies to cover a shopkeeper for any losses incurred if he were robbed—money, medical bills, damages, and so forth. But since there was very little crime, the premiums were quite low, and most people carried insurance. People had a good bit of free cash, since there were no taxes, and therefore they were able not only to buy adequate insurance, but to send their children to private schools, and to buy police protection as well.

Generally, the police forces were subsidiaries of the insurance companies, a natural enough development. After all, the better a company could protect its clients, the more clients it would have, and the fewer claims it would have to pay. At the same time, if a crime was committed, the criminal had to be caught, lest he do it again and further eat into profits. The pay of this force of private investigators, therefore, was based upon its efficiency in apprehending criminal elements; this guaranteed a high measure of success, even as an investigator's complete responsibility for his personal actions assured his care in protecting the rights of innocent parties. These private police officers were well respected, and, ironically, it was the very criminals they caught who paid them. The system was, like most other things in Anartopia, based simply on common sense.

If a bank were to be robbed of ten kilograms of gold, the bandit was aware that if he were caught, he would be held responsible for repayment of the stolen property, and that damages, including compensation for any injuries or death he caused, would also be adjudicated and levied on him. In addition, he would have to pay for his own trial, as well as the time and risk of the police officer. If he were found guilty of the crime, a bill for the total was presented to him for disposal. It was a system in which, truly, crime did not pay.

The accused could choose from any number of independent arbitration agencies for his trial, and the insurance company, or the injured, could accept or reject his choice; sometimes the two agents would collaborate in choosing a third to try the case. Since no individual court had a monopoly on justice, the courts competed on the basis of the fairness and the intelligence of their decisions.

Should the accused be found innocent, he had recourse against the insurance company or police force who had accused him; if he were found guilty, he had to pay his total debt—not to society, which was an archaic and meaningless non-entity—but to those to whom he had caused loss. Payment was assured by various compensation houses.

The compensation houses were operated for a profit, of course, and competed on the basis of their efficiency in recovering losses through production by their inmates: a brilliant counterfeiter might be employed as a printer; a con artist might do well as a salesman—under close supervision; a derelict would be trained to do whatever he was best suited for, to pay off his incurred debt soonest. Since sentences given were in terms of grams of gold, not years, everyone generally worked hard in order to regain his freedom as soon as possible. As inmates showed both a willingness and ability to make good, they were usually released on their own recognizance, because compensation houses were in business to make money, not imprison people.

The country's socio–economic system (or as some said, its "lack of a political system") allowed people freedom to do as they deemed best in the present, and gave them the certainty needed to plan for the future. The business of Anartopia was business, and business was good.

Very often, people from other lands would visit Anartopia to see how conditions were. Most people liked the place and wanted to come there to live, which was, as a rule, fine with existing residents. Newcomers got no special treatment, just the opportunity to provide goods and services the way everyone else did, and should an immigrant prove incapable of doing so, his landlord would simply evict him for non–payment of the rent. Since absolutely everything, including the street, was privately owned, a moocher then had no choice but to return whence he came—if he was still welcome there. Generally, though, the newcomers were among the brightest and most productive in their own homelands, and as such, brought many valuable skills to Anartopia. Unemployment was never a problem, since everybody had an infinite desire for more goods and services. A man could work twenty–four hours a day, providing he found a way to do without sleep.

Some immigrants' homelands were plagued by such phenomena as air and water pollution, and most Anartopians lived near the center of the country, because, unfortunately, the borders set up by the other countries could not contain their waste products. (The Anartopians could not see why anyone needed borders with guard posts and barbed wire, anyway. Everyone simply marked off his property, and that was sufficient.) In Anartopia, a man with a belching smokestack found himself in jeopardy for polluting his neighbor's air, thereby violating his property rights; it was, therefore, cheaper, easier, and better public relations to insure smokestacks did not pollute. Rivers were all privately owned, although sometimes by cooperatives of their shoreowners, and the owners no more would pollute their rivers than they would build a trash heap in their backyards; of course, they had a right to, but it was not good sense, and people who did pollute the river were charged fees by the owners. Some rivers were cleaner than others, depending on what was most profitable, but a person could swim in all of them.

In general, though, people did not worry about any of this. The free market took care of itself, and everyone got on very nicely, as long as he minded his own business.

THE BEGINNING OF THE END

One day, in the part of the region east of the mountains (the country of Dystopia, that is), a bright young fellow named Leviathan was contemplating how to make things even better. He had traveled outside of Anartopia and noted that in other countries, "the public good" was always placed above the private good; the public good was provided for by an institution known as "government." Certainly, he reasoned, if this philosophy was inculcated into his already prosperous country, things would be better yet. Just as it took good planning to build a house, it also took good planning to build a nation. Most Anartopians did not want a nation, however; they just wanted a place to live. Or at least, that is what they thought they wanted. The trouble with most people, of course, was that they did not really know what they wanted, and the determination of that, Leviathan decided, would be one of the first duties of the new government.

At first, Leviathan took the direct approach in securing the benefits of a government for his fellow citizens. He retained a couple of bully boys, dressed them in khaki uniforms, and sent them out to extract tribute in order to pay their salaries, as well as his own. The scenario was appealing in its simplicity, and seemed, actually, to fulfill the most important function of most governments young Leviathan had seen. His boys would only have to go out, announce to a given resident that they represented the new government in the area, and as such, had decided to levy a tax.

When they tried it, however, they were immediately locked up as common criminals. Leviathan knew there had to be a better way, and he was back to the drawing board. In his first attempt at politics, our young statesman had confused what governments do with how they are started.

The astute application of mass psychology succeeded where direct coercion failed. Every citizen, deep in his heart, knew he could mind his neighbor's business better than his neighbor could. He could do so because he was in a position to be "objective" in determining "priorities," whereas the neighbor was so involved in his own life, he often could not be depended upon to act in his own best interest. Oddly enough, though, whenever a chap did act in his own interest, it was only because he was "selfish," and somehow that did not seem right, either. Leviathan was quick to capitalize on this insight; the solution seemed to lie in passing laws and regulations—the second function of government. The need for some form of regulation was especially apparent to those who felt they would be called upon to do the regulating, and Leviathan's ideas moved from the idle chatter of cocktail parties to the headlines of newspapers and the megaphones of public rallies.

Leviathan industriously explained to the citizens of Anartopia the advantages of government. Under the New, Improved Government (since that previous attempt at government had not met with approval in the marketplace), everyone would have his say in how things were run. Everyone knew of something (or someone) they did not like, which might be eliminated, or something they would liked, that could be created. Clearly, a government was a great way to get everyone else to pay for the changes that were needed; and soon ideas and suggestions on how to use the new government were pouring in.

Housewives felt bakers should charge less for their bread; bakers thought farmers should charge less for their wheat; farmers lobbied against the fertilizer companies; and the fertilizer companies asked for wage controls on their workers. Of course, in response, the workers' wives redoubled their efforts to roll back the price of bread.

Tenants felt landlords should charge less, and looked to the heralded government to put a ceiling on rents; landlords asked for zoning laws to prevent "overbuilding," since competition reduced their profits.

Growers of apples believed they could get the government to buy their product at higher than market prices; consumers of apples believed they could get the government to sell its grower–induced surplus of apples at less than market prices. Both groups, of course, were proven right. It was wonderful!

Businessmen saw profitable new contracts; workers saw soft new jobs. Consumers (a newly formed class of people) saw protection from the marketplace. There was something for everyone. Confidence and optimism were the order of the day; stock prices rose.

Those who wanted to be elected vied for an office in the new government by promising something for nothing, or at least something for a vote. Never–never land lay at the end of the yellow brick road, and the new government would build it—along with all the other roads.

Elections were held, and a good number of citizens pledged to spend their time, and others' money, in making sure everyone received according to his needs. It was determined that each should pay for these marvels according to his ability, and the bully boys from the earlier government were called upon for their expertise in collecting. They were not only pleased at the opportunity to ply their trade with impunity, but the time they had spent in jail making reparations for their last foray left them in a fine humor to do so. And if a bank, insurance company, or police force was desirous of being granted its now–necessary licenses, it would do well to recognize that its first obligation was to the government, not its own clients. Indeed, contracts for protection were rewritten to exclude the government (or the "State") as a defendant in claims. It became academic when they all merged into the government because of the inefficiency of "cutthroat competition" and "duplication of services." As a consequence, services became either inefficient or nonexistent.

The regulatory and legislative functions of government were great fun, but the resulting taxes were a bit ticklish, since no one really wanted to pay them. This reluctance was overcome to some degree when the government started offering bounties to public–spirited citizens who turned in those who were shirking. Previously, no one had cared whether his neighbor shirked, since that meant only that the neighbor himself suffered. Now that everyone was pulling together in a common cause, however, there was good reason to worry about these things. Poorer people complained that richer people, since they had more, should pay more. The rich patronized the legislators (indeed, they usually *were* the legislators) to ensure they would pay less. In order to make the poorer people happy, though, the government provided free bread, circuses, and medical care. And just so that everyone got something, the middle class was given higher taxes.

Gold was used to pay the taxes, and this presented another problem. The metal was easy to hide from the government and, therefore, it usually was hidden, not placed on deposit with banks. Also, it was universally acceptable, which meant it would often leave the country through the newly erected borders. In any event, soon there was not enough, and the government was called on to make available more money. They created the "dreck," as a new form of money. It was accepted within Dystopia mainly because one had to accept it; it was accepted outside of Dystopia either because there were goods inside Dystopia for which it could be traded (other than gold, of course), or because foreigners simply did not know any better. In the national interest, the government confiscated everyone's gold in order to fill the national treasury; most people acquiesced, since the treasury gave them drecks in return, which were as good as gold. In fact, the dreck was better than gold, because one could make as many of them as desired, and needless to say, everybody wanted many of them. Since the government now could create money, it had to expropriate less from the citizens in the form of taxes, which decreased. Stock prices rose again; but the price of everything else increased, too. The price increases were termed "inflation." Nobody knew where it came from, but everyone still thought that lots of money meant lots of prosperity, so they created more money in hope of creating prosperity. For some reason, though, prosperity was in short supply—along with many other things.

As time went on, some of the poor stopped working, and used the time instead to campaign for more freebies, which they usually got. Taxes started moving up again, and that threw others out of work, because now people had less money (after taxes and inflation). Increasingly, they lived on stores of wealth they had put away when things were better. More people spent their time petitioning the government to soak the rich (whose ranks they increasingly despaired of joining anyway), or to hire more police to defend them from the poor (whose ranks they increasingly feared joining), or to regulate the middle class (in whose ranks everyone was afraid to admit membership). After all, if the government would not take care of these inequities, what was it there for? The legislators did not wish to be considered remiss in their duties, and redoubled their efforts to build a better system, or "New Order."

Armed with their newly acquired hoard of gold and their increasing powers, the legislators were like so many drunken but benevolent sailors storming ashore with a year's pay. The stock market rose again, even as Dystopia became a post–industrial state.

And there were other benefits. The government now could do more than ever to establish new frontiers, and to build a much–needed, great society. Artists were commissioned to immortalize the politicians who hired them; builders commemorated noble ideals in public monuments, as well as in public housing and public works. Everyone approved of science, so projects were found for scientists to keep them off the streets and welfare rolls. Some were sent to study the mating calls of toads (they spent only 20,324 drecks to gain a definitive view). On another project, 19,300 drecks were spent to find out that children fell off their tricycles because of "unstable performance, particularly rollover while turning." One chap had a fine junket to Burma with 8,000 drecks, to hunt for a particular species of ant. And as society started to break down in Dystopia, it was deemed wise to spend 154,000 drecks to teach mothers how to play with their babies. [1]

In spite of all these fine efforts, though, industry was flagging, and needed stimulation. It was revived by offering foreign countries drecks, on the condition they would use them to buy goods from Dystopian industry. Railroads and shipping lines found prosperity crating and boxing the accumulated substance of Dystopia in exchange for the drecks their government had given foreigners. Many of the better class of Dystopians left in disgust, and made their way across the mountains to Anarchia.

Things looked especially promising to those who stayed, though, as a war was fomented. The enemy was declared to be the area of land over the mountains that had not opted for participation in the New, Improved Government due to a general lack of interest; now-President Leviathan felt they would be an excellent first target, since they had no army. The ostensible reason for the war was that the Anarchians were stealing citizens from Dystopia, and theft of government property was a serious offense.

The war solved many problems. It solved unemployment, since everyone not working in a "strategic industry" was drafted. It solved the disuse of factories whose products people could no longer afford, since they could be turned to the production of weapons (which people still could not afford). Not only did the nation suddenly "need" weapons, but better yet, they would always have to be replaced as the enemy blew them up. Indeed, if the government conducted the war with anything approaching the skill with which it ran the country, the factories would run around the clock making new weapons. Pundits hailed the way everyone pulled together, like it or not, in a common effort to devastate their erstwhile friends.

And it was great sport besides. Rumor had it (news being censored) that the Anarchians had great amounts of wealth—refrigerators, autos, color TV sets, food, gold—and

---

[1] None of this would be particularly noteworthy, except that years earlier, identical amounts (in dollars, of course) had already been spent on these projects by the U.S. government.

the Dystopians were anxious to get these things to improve their standard of living, which had been slipping inexplicably for some time. Actually, the Dystopians were more than willing to pay the Anarchians for what they wanted, but the latter would not accept drecks. That was because the dreck was good only in Dystopia, and Dystopian products were deemed of high price and inferior quality (except for their bombs, tanks, and such, which nobody wanted in the first place).

The war against the Anarchians did not go as well as might have been hoped, though. When the army arrived in a city, the people looked at the tanks as curiosity pieces, and moved out of the way as they rumbled through. There was no resistance, and though there was laughter at the robot–like way the Dystopian soldiers walked, the natives were actually friendly and accommodating, until the soldiers indicated why they had come. It was at that point that Dystopian soldiers started disappearing from the streets at night when they were alone or in small groups. Morale became low; desertions were high; and the better class of soldier sympathized with the "enemy."

Armies do best fighting enemies they hate, not oppressing people they like and respect. The Dystopian government was disturbed at these developments. The chance for fighting, though, came soon enough: a third country attacked the capital of Dystopia and leveled half of it in the ensuing fray. This stroke of good fortune imbued the soldiers with the will to kill; they bid a fond farewell to Anarchia to devastate their new enemy.

The two warring governments succeeded handsomely in mutual destruction, even as they had done in self–destruction of their homelands. President Leviathan reveled in this discovery of government's third function, even as organized society in Dystopia ceased to exist.

The Anarchians, however, were sad to see all of this transpire, since it meant it would be years before the Dystopians had any real wealth with which to trade them for the many goods they had in surplus. But they helped how they could, by hiring displaced and unemployed Dystopians (which was most of them). They found the Dystopians had skills only in fighting, political organizing, receiving welfare, or making tanks, but since there was no government in Anarchia, there was no demand for those skills, and they all had to be retrained. Meanwhile, the Dystopian stock market reached new heights as the dreck became totally worthless, and even a billion of them would not buy a share in the typically bankrupt company.

Anarchian charities (they could afford charities, since they were not only eager producers but "miserly hoarders") staved off famine in the land, while businessmen lent Dystopian farmers seeds and tools—at a handsome profit— in order to provide for themselves the next year. The Dystopians were grateful, as they should have been, and both parties grew richer, as is always the case when people trade freely.

Some grayheads remembered the days before the cornucopia was discovered, and wondered why the country was in ruins. Where went all the wealth that had been created by their forefathers over decades? A bomb crater, a welfare check stub, a deserted building, a public monument, a public housing project, and a public works building all gave a clue.

Perhaps a more direct answer could have been given by President Leviathan, or some of the legislators. If so, however, they would have been given time in court to explain in full—and would have had years working in restitution at the "public service" jobs they were assigned, during which they could contemplate their answers.

The stock market moved ahead once more, though this time in terms of gold.

Sauve qui peut.
("Let him who can, save himself.")

Douglas Casey graduated from Georgetown University in 1968, and has written a number of best–selling books. *Crisis Investing* (Harper & Row, 1979) became the largest selling financial book in history. Casey's other books include *The International Man* and *Strategic Investing*. He was co–chair of the 1996 campaign of Libertarian Party Presidential candidate Harry Browne. His website is www.CaseyResearch.com.

CHAPTER 4

THE DEATH OF POLITICS

By Karl Hess

This is not a time of radical, revolutionary politics. Not yet.

Unrest, riot, dissent, and chaos notwithstanding, today's politics is reactionary. Both right and left are reactionary and authoritarian. That is to say: both are political. They seek only to revise current methods of acquiring and wielding political power. Radical and revolutionary movements seek not to revise but to revoke. The target of revocation should be obvious. The target is politics itself.

Radicals and revolutionaries have had their sights trained on politics for some time. As governments fail around the world, as more millions become aware that government never has and never can humanely and effectively manage men's affairs, government's own inadequacy will emerge, at last, as the basis for a truly radical and revolutionary movement. In the meantime, the radical–revolutionary position is a lonely one. It is feared or hated, by both the right and left—although both right and left must borrow from it to survive. The radical–revolutionary position is libertarianism, and its socio-economic form is laissez–faire capitalism.

Libertarianism is the view that each man is the absolute owner of his life, to use and dispose of as he sees fit; that all man's social actions should be voluntary; and that respect for every other man's similar and equal ownership of life and, by extension, the property and fruits of that life, is the ethical basis of a humane and open society. In this view, the only—repeat: only—function of law or government is to provide the sort of self–defense against violence that an individual, if he were powerful enough, would provide for himself.

If it were not for the fact that libertarianism freely concedes the right of men voluntarily to form communities or governments on the same ethical basis, libertarianism could be called anarchy.

Laissez–faire capitalism, or anarcho-capitalism, is simply the economic form of the libertarian ethic. Laissez–faire capitalism encompasses the notion that men should exchange goods and services, without regulation, solely on the basis of value for value. It recognizes charity and communal enterprises as voluntary versions of this same ethic. Such a system would be straight barter, except for the widely felt need for a division of labor in which men, voluntarily, accept value tokens such as cash and credit. Economically, this system is anarchy, and proudly so.

Libertarianism is rejected by the modern left—which preaches individualism but practices collectivism. Capitalism is rejected by the modern right—which preaches enterprise but practices protectionism. The libertarian faith in the mind of man is rejected by religionists who have faith only in the sins of man. The libertarian insistence that men be free to spin cables of steel as well as dreams of smoke is rejected by hippies who adore nature but spurn creation. The libertarian insistence that each man is a sovereign land of liberty, with his primary allegiance to himself, is rejected by patriots who sing of freedom but "also shout of banners and boundaries. There is no operating political movement in the world today that is based upon a libertarian philosophy. If there were, it would be in the anomalous position of using political power to abolish political power.

Perhaps a regular political movement, overcoming this anomaly, will actually develop. Believe it or not, there were strong possibilities of such a development in the 1964 Presidential campaign of Barry Goldwater. Underneath the scary headlines, Goldwater hammered away at such purely political structures as the military draft, general taxation, censorship, nationalism, legislated conformity, political establishment of social norms, and war as an instrument of international policy.

It is true that, in a common political paradox, Goldwater (a major general in the Air Force Reserve) has spoken of reducing state power while at the same time advocating the increase of state power to fight the Cold War. He is not a pacifist. He believes that war remains an acceptable state action. He does not see the Cold War as involving U.S. imperialism. He sees it as a result only of Soviet imperialism. Time after time, however, he has said that economic pressure, diplomatic negotiation, and the persuasions of propaganda (or "cultural warfare") are absolutely preferable to violence. He has also said that antagonistic ideologies can "never be beaten by bullets, but only by better ideas."

A defense of Goldwater cannot be carried too far, however. His domestic libertarian tendencies simply do not carry over into his view of foreign policy. Libertarianism, unalloyed, is absolutely isolationist, in that it is absolutely opposed to the institutions of national government that are the only agencies on earth now able to wage war or intervene in foreign affairs.

In other campaign issues, however, the libertarian coloration in the Goldwater complexion was more distinct. The fact that he roundly rapped the fiscal irresponsibility of Social Security before an elderly audience, and the fact that he criticized the Tennessee Valley Authority (TVA) while speaking in Tennessee, were not examples of political naïveté. They simply showed Goldwater's high disdain for politics itself, summed up in his campaign statement that people would be told "what they need to hear and not what they want to hear."

There was also some suggestion of libertarianism in the campaign of Eugene McCarthy, in his splendid attacks on Presidential power. However, these were canceled out by his vague, but nevertheless perceptible, defense of government power in general. There was virtually no suggestion of libertarianism in the statements of any other politician during that year's campaign.

I was a speech writer for Barry Goldwater in the 1964 campaign.

During the campaign, I recall very clearly, there was a moment, at a conference to determine the campaign's "farm strategy," when a respected and very conservative Senator arose to say, "Barry, you've got to make it clear that you believe that the American farmer has a right to a decent living."

Senator Goldwater replied, with the tact for which he was renowned, "But he doesn't have a right to it. Neither do I. We just have a right to try for it." And that was the end of that.

Now, in contrast, take Tom Hayden of, at that time, Students for a Democratic Society. Writing in *The Radical Papers,* he said that his "revolution" sought "institutions outside the established order." One of those institutions, he amplified, would be "people's own antipoverty organizations fighting for federal money."

Of the two men, which is radical or revolutionary? Hayden said, in effect, that he simply wants to bulldoze his way into the establishment. Goldwater said he wants, in effect, to topple it, to forever end its power to advantage or disadvantage anyone.

This is not to defend the Goldwater Presidential campaign as libertarian. It is only to say that his campaign contained a healthy element of this sort of radicalism. But otherwise, the Goldwater campaign was very deeply in hock to regular partisan interests, images, myths, and manners.

In foreign policy, particularly, there arises a great impediment to the emergence of a libertarian wing in either of the major political parties. Men who call upon the end of state authority in every other area insist upon its being maintained to build a war machine with which to hold the Communists at bay. It is only lately that the imperatives of logic—and the emergence of antistatist forces in eastern Europe—have begun to make it more acceptable to ask whether the garrison state needed to maintain the Cold War might not be as bad as or worse than the punitive threat being guarded against. Goldwater has not taken and never did take such a revisionist line—but, among Cold Warriors, his disposition to libertarian principles makes him more susceptible than most.

GOD OF MODERN LIBERALISM

This is not merely a digression on behalf of a political figure (almost an antipolitical figure) whom I profoundly respect. It is, rather, to emphasize the inadequacy of traditional, popular guidelines in assessing the reactionary nature of contemporary politics and in divining the true nature of radical and revolutionary antipolitics. Political parties and politicians today—all parties and all politicians—question only the forms through which they will express their common belief in controlling the lives of others. Power, particularly majoritarian or collective power (*i.e.*, the power of an elite, exercised in the name of the masses), is the god of the modern liberal. Its only recent innovative change is to suggest that the elite be leavened by the compulsory membership of authentic representatives of the masses. The current phrase is "participatory democracy."

Just as power is the god of the modern liberal, God remains the authority of the modern conservative. Liberalism practices regimentation by, simply, regimentation. Conservatism practices regimentation by, not quite so simply, revelation. But regimented or revealed, the name of the game is still politics.

The great flaw in conservatism is a deep fissure down which talk of freedom falls, to be dashed to death on the rocks of authoritarianism. Conservatives worry that the state has too much power over people. But it was conservatives who gave the state that power. It was conservatives, very similar to today's conservatives, who ceded to the state the power to produce not simply order in the community, but *a certain kind of order.*

It was European conservatives who, apparently fearful of the openness of the Industrial Revolution (why, *anyone* could get rich!), struck the first blows at capitalism by encouraging and accepting laws that made the disruptions of innovation and competition less frequent and eased the way for the comforts and collusions of cartelization.

Big business in America today, and for some years past, has been openly at war with competition and, thus, at war with laissez–faire capitalism. Big business supports a form of state capitalism in which government and big business act as partners. Criticism of this statist bent of big business comes more often from the left than from the right, and this is another factor making it difficult to tell the players apart. John Kenneth Galbraith, for instance, has taken big business to task for its anticompetitive mentality. The right, meantime, blissfully defends big business as though it had not, in fact, become just the sort of bureaucratic, authoritarian force that rightists reflexively attack when it is governmental.

The left's attack on corporate capitalism is an attack on economic forms possible only in a collusion between authoritarian government and bureaucratized, non-entre-preneurial business. It is unfortunate that many New Leftists are so uncritical as to accept this premise as indicating that all forms of capitalism are bad, so that full state ownership is the only alternative. This thinking has its mirror image on the right.

It was American conservatives, for instance, who very early in the game gave up the fight against state franchising and regulation, and, instead, embraced state regulation for their own special advantage. Conservatives today continue to revere the state as an instrument of chastisement, even as they reject it as an instrument of beneficence. The conservative who wants a federally authorized prayer in the classroom is the same conservative who objects to federally authorized textbooks in the classroom.

Murray Rothbard, writing in *Ramparts,* has summed up this flawed conservatism in describing a "new, younger generation of rightists, of 'conservatives'...who thought that the real problem of the modern world was nothing so ideological as the state vs. individual liberty or government intervention vs. the free market; the real problem, they declared, was the preservation of tradition, order, Christianity and good manners against the modern sins of reason, license, atheism and boorishness."

The reactionary tendencies of both liberals and conservatives today show clearly in their willingness to cede, to the state or the community, power far beyond the protection of liberty against violence. For differing purposes, both see the state as an instrument not protecting man's freedom, but either instructing or restricting how that freedom is to be used.

Once the power of the community becomes in any sense normative, rather than merely protective, it is difficult to see where any lines may be drawn to limit further trans-gressions against individual freedom. In fact, the lines have not been drawn. They will never be drawn by political parties that argue merely the cost of programs or institutions founded on state power. Actually, the lines can be drawn only by a radical questioning of power itself, and by the libertarian vision that sees man as capable of moving on without the encumbering luggage of laws and politics that do not merely preserve man's right to his life, but attempt, in addition, to tell him how to live it.

For many conservatives, the bad dream that haunts their lives and their political position (which many sum up as "law and order") is one of riot. To my knowledge, there is no limit that conservatives would place upon the power of the state to suppress riots.

Even in a laissez–faire society, of course, the right to self–defense would have to be assumed, and a place for self–defense on a community basis could easily be imagined. But community self–defense would always be exclusively defensive. Conservatives betray an easy willingness to believe that the state should also initiate certain *offensive* actions, in order to preclude trouble later on. "Getting tough" is the phrase most often used. It does not mean just getting tough on rioters. It means getting tough on entire ranges of attitudes: clipping long hair, rousting people from parks for carrying concealed guitars, stopping and questioning anyone who doesn't look like a member of the Jaycees, drafting all the ne'er–do–wells to straighten them up, ridding our theaters and bookstores of "filth," and, always and above all, putting "those" people in their place. To the conservative, all too often, the alternatives are social conformity or unthinkable chaos.

Even if these were the only alternatives—which they obviously aren't—there are many reasons for preferring chaos to conformity. Personally, I believe I would have a better chance of surviving with a Watts, Chicago, Detroit, or Washington in flames than with an entire nation snug in a garrison.

Riots in modern America must be broken down into component parts. They are not all simple looting and violence against life and property. They are also directed against the prevailing violence of the state—the sort of on–going civic violence that permits regular police supervision of everyday life in some neighborhoods, the rules and regulations that inhibit absolutely free trading, the public schools that serve the visions of bureaucracy rather than the varieties of individual people. There is violence also by those who simply want to shoot their way into political power otherwise denied them. Conservatives seem to think that greater state police power is the answer. Liberals seem to think that more preferential state welfare power is the answer. Power, power, power.

Except for ordinary looters—for whom the answer must be to stop them as you would any other thief—the real answer to rioting must lie elsewhere. It must lie in the abandonment, not the extension, of state power—state power that oppresses people, state power that tempts people. To cite one strong example: the white stores in many black neighborhoods, which are said to cause such dissatisfaction and envy, have a special, unrealized advantage, thanks to state power. In a very poor neighborhood there may be many with the natural ability to open a retail store, but it is much less likely that these people would also have the ability to meet all the state and city regulations, governing everything from cleanliness to bookkeeping, which very often comprise the marginal difference between going into business or staying out. In a real laissez–faire society, the local entrepreneur, with whom the neighbors might prefer to deal, could go openly into business—selling marijuana, whiskey, numbers slips, books, food, or medical advice from the trunk of his car. He could forget about ledgers, forms and reports, and simply get on with the business of business, rather than the business of bureaucracy. Allowing ghetto dwellers to compete on their own terms, rather than on someone else's, should prove a more satisfying and practical solution to ghetto problems than either rampages or restrictions.

The libertarian thrusts away from power and authority that marked the Goldwater campaign were castigated from the left as being "nostalgic yearnings for a simpler world." (Perhaps akin to the simplistic yearnings of the hippies whom the left so easily tolerates, even while it excoriates Goldwater.) Goldwater's libertarianism was castigated from the right—he received virtually *no* support from big business—as representing policies that could lead to unregulated competition, international free trade, and even worse, a weakening of the very special partnership that big business now enjoys with Big Government.

The most incredible convolution in the thinking that attacked Goldwater as reactionary, which he wasn't, rather than radical, which he was, came in regard to nuclear weapons. In that area, he was specifically damned for daring to propose that the control of these weapons be shared, and even proposing they be placed fully in the multinational command of the North Atlantic Treaty Organization, rather than left to the personal, one-man discretion of the President of the United States.

Again, who is reactionary and who is radical? The men who want an atomic king enthroned in Washington, or the man who dares ask that that divine right of destruction become less divine and more divided? Until recently, it was a popular cocktail pastime to speculate on the difference between the war in Vietnam under "Save–the–world–from–Goldwater" Johnson, or as it might have been under wild Barry, who, by his every campaign utterance, would have been bound to share the Vietnam decision (and the fighting) with NATO, rather than simply and unilaterally going it alone.

A CIVIL RIGHTS MOVEMENT

To return to the point: the most vital question today about politics—not *in* politics—is the same sort of question that is plaguing Christianity. Superficially, the Christian question seems simply what kind of religion should be chosen. But basically, the question is whether any irrational or mystical forces are supportable, as a way to order society, in a world increasingly able and ready to be rational. The political version of the question may be stated this way: will men continue to submit to rule by politics, which has always meant the power of some men over other men, or are we ready to do it alone socially, in communities of voluntarism, in a world more economic and cultural than political, just as so many now are prepared to go it alone metaphysically, in a world more of reason than religion?

The radical and revolutionary answer that a libertarian, laissez–faire position gives to that question is not quite anarchy. The libertarian, laissez–faire movement is actually, if embarrassingly for some, a civil rights movement. But it is antipolitical, in that it builds diversified power to be protected against government, even to dispense with government to a major degree, rather than seeking power to protect government or to perform any special social purpose.

It is a civil–liberties movement, in that it seeks civil liberties, for everyone, as defined in the nineteenth century by William Graham Sumner, one of Yale's first professors of political and social science. Sumner said: "Civil liberty is the status of the man who is guaranteed by law and civil institutions the exclusive employment of all his own powers for his own welfare."

Modern liberals, of course, would call this selfishness, and they would be correct, with intense emphasis on "self." Many modern conservatives would say that they agree with Sumner, but they would not be correct. Men who call themselves conservatives, but who operate in the larger industries, spend considerable time, and not a small amount of money, fighting government subsidies to labor unions (in the form of welfare programs). They do not fight *direct* subsidies to industries—such as transportation, farming, or universities. They do not, in short, believe that men are entitled to the exclusive employment of their own powers for their own welfare, because they accept the practice of taxing a good part of that power to use for the welfare of other people.

As noted, for all the theoretical screaming that sometimes may be heard from the industrial right, it is safe to say that the major powers of government to regulate industry were derived not only from the support of businessmen, but actually at the insistence of businessmen. Uneconomical mail rates are cherished by businessmen who can profit from them and who, significantly, seem uninterested in the obvious possibility of transforming the postal service from a bureau into a business. As a business, of course, it would charge what it costs to mail things, not what is simply convenient for users to pay.

The big businessmen who operate the major broadcast networks are not known for suggesting, as a laissez–faire concept would insist, that competition for channels and audiences be wide open and unregulated. As a consequence, of course, the networks get all the government control that they deserve, accepting it in good cheer because, even if censored, they are also protected from competition. It is notable, also, that one of the most fierce denunciations of pay TV (which, under capitalism, should be a conceptual commonplace) came not from the *Daily Worker,* but from the *Reader's Digest,* that supposed bastion of conservatism. Actually, I think the *Digest* is such a bastion. It seems to believe that the state is an institution divinely ordained to make men moral—in a "Judaeo–Christian" sense, of course. It abhors, as does no publication short of William Buckley's *National Review,* the insolence of those untidy persons who today so regularly challenge the authority of the state.

In short, there is no evidence whatsoever that modern conservatives subscribe to the "your life is your own" philosophy upon which libertarianism is founded. An interesting illustration that conservatism not only disagrees with libertarianism, but is downright hostile to it, is that the most widely known libertarian author of the day, Miss Ayn Rand, ranks only a bit below, or slightly to the side of, Leonid Brezhnev, as an object of diatribe in *National Review.* Specifically, it seems, she is reviled on the right because she is an atheist, daring to take exception to the *National Review* notion that man's basically evil nature (stemming from original sin) means he must be held in check by a strong and authoritarian social order.

Barry Goldwater, during his 1964 campaign, repeatedly said that "the government strong enough to give you what you want is strong enough to take it all away." Conservatives, as a group, have forgotten, or prefer to ignore, that this also applies to government's strength to impose social order. If government can enforce social norms, or even Christian behavior, it can also take away or twist them.

To repeat: conservatives yearn for a state, or "leadership," with the power to restore order and to put things—and people—back in their places. They yearn for political power. Liberals yearn for a state that will bomb the rich and balm the poor. They, too, yearn for political power. Libertarians yearn for a state that cannot, beyond any possibility of amendment, confer any advantage on anyone; a state that cannot compel anything, but simply prevents the use of violence, in place of other exchanges, in relationships between individuals or groups.

Such a state would have as its sole purpose (probably supported exclusively by use taxes or fees) the maintenance of a system to adjudicate disputes (courts), to protect citizens against violence (police), to maintain some form of currency for ease of commerce, and, as long as it might be needed because of the existence of national borders and differences, to maintain a defense force. Meanwhile, libertarians should also work to end the whole concept of the nation–state itself. The major point here is that libertarians would start with no outstanding predispositions about public functions, being disposed always to think that there is in the personal and private world of individuals someone who can or will come along with a solution that gets the job done, without conferring upon anyone power that has not been earned through voluntary exchange.

In fact, it is in the matters most appropriate to collective interest—such as courts and protection against violence— that government today often defaults. This follows the bureaucratic tendency to perform least–needed services— where the risk of accountability is minimal—and to avoid performing essential but highly accountable services. Courts are clogged beyond belief. Police, rather than simply protecting citizens against violence, are deeply involved in overseeing private morals. In black neighborhoods particularly, the police serve as unloved, and unwanted, arbiters of everyday life.

If, in the past few paragraphs, the reader can detect any hint of a position that would be compatible with either the Communist Party of the Soviet Union or the National Association of Manufacturers, he is strongly advised to look again. No such common ground exists. Nor can any common ground be adduced in terms of "new politics" versus "old politics." New or old, the positions that parade today under these titles are still politics and, like roses, they smell alike. Radical and revolutionary politicians— antipoliticians, if you will—should be able to sniff them out easily.

Specific matters that illustrate the differences would

include the draft, marijuana, monopoly, censorship, isolationism–internationalism, race relations, and urban affairs, to name a few.

As part of his aborted campaign for the Presidency, Nelson Rockefeller took a position on the draft. In it, he specifically took exception to Richard Nixon's draft stand, calling it the "old politics" as contrasted with his own "new politics." The Rockefeller position involved a certain streamlining of the draft, but nothing that would change it from what it patently is—forced, involuntary servitude. Rockefeller criticized Nixon for having asserted that, someday, the draft could be replaced by a voluntary system, an old Republican promise.

The new politician contended that the Nixon system wouldn't work because it never *had* worked. The fact that this nation has never offered to pay its soldiers at a rate realistic enough to attract them was not covered in Rockefeller's statement. Nor did the new politician address himself to the fact that, given a nation which not enough citizens can be attracted to defend voluntarily, you probably also have a nation which, by definition, isn't really worth defending.

The old politician, on the other hand, did not present quite as crisp a position on the draft as the new politician tried to pin him with. Nixon, although theoretically in favor of a voluntary military, was—along with the presumably even *more* conservative Ronald Reagan—opposed to trying voluntarism until *after* the Vietnam War. Throughout the conservative stance, one sees a repetition of this position. Freedom is fine—but it must be deferred as long as a hot war or the Cold War has to be fought.

All should be struck by the implications of that baleful notion. It implies that free men simply cannot be ingenious enough to defend themselves against violence without themselves becoming violent—not toward the enemy alone, but to their own persons and liberty as well. If our freedom is so fragile that it must be continuously protected by giving it up, then we are in deep trouble. And, in fact, by following a somewhat similar course, we got ourselves in very deep trouble in Southeast Asia. The Johnson war there was escalated precisely on the belief that South Vietnam's freedom may best be obtained by dictating what form of government it should have—day by day, even—and by defending it against the North Vietnamese by devastating the southern countryside.

In foreign relations, as in domestic pronouncements, new and old politicians preach the same dusty doctrines of compulsion and contradiction. The radical preachment of libertarianism, the antipolitical preachment, would be that as long as the inanity of war between nation–states remains a possibility, free nation–states will at least protect themselves from wars by hiring volunteers, not by murdering voluntarism.

GREAT COMIC FIGURE

One of the most medievally fascinating minds of the twentieth century, that of Lewis Hershey, sole owner and proprietor of the Selective Service System, has put this unpretty picture into perfect perspective with his memorable statement, delivered at a National Press Club luncheon, that he "hate[s] to think of the day that [his] grandchildren would be defended by volunteers." There, in as ugly an example as is on public record, is precisely where politics and power, authority and the arthritis of traditionalism, are bound to take you. Director Hershey is prevented from being a great comic figure by the rather obvious fact that, being involved with the deaths of so many unwilling men, and imprisonment of so many others, he becomes a tragic figure, or at least, a figure in a tragedy. There is no new or old politics about the draft. A draft is political, plain and simple. A volunteer military is essentially commercial. And it is between politics and commerce that the entrant into radical or revolutionary politics must continually choose.

Marijuana is an example of such a choice. In a laissez–faire society, there could exist no public institution with the power to forcefully protect people from themselves. From other people (criminals), yes. From one's own self, no. Marijuana is a plant, a crop. People who smoke it do not do so under the compulsion either of physiological addiction or of institutionalized power. They do so voluntarily. They find a person who has volunteered to grow it. They agree on a price. One sells; the other buys. One acquires new capital;

the other acquires a euphoric experience that, he decides, was worth allocating some of his own resources to obtain.

Nowhere in the equation is there a single point at which the neighbors, or any multitude of neighbors, posing as priesthood or public, have the slightest rational reason to intervene. The action has not, in any way, deprived anyone else of "the exclusive employment of all his own powers for his own welfare."

The current laws against marijuana, in contravention even of all available medical evidence regarding its nature, are a prime example of the use of political power. The very power that makes it possible for the state to ban marijuana, and to arrest Lenny Bruce, is the same power that makes it possible for the state to exact taxes from one man to pay into the pockets of another. The purpose may seem different, but upon examination they are not. Marijuana must be banned to prevent people from succumbing to the madness of its fumes and doing some mischief upon the community. Poverty, too, must be banned for a similar reason. Poor people, unless made unpoor, will angrily rise and do mischief upon the community. As in all politics, purpose and power blend and reinforce each other.

"Hard" narcotics must be subject to the same test as marijuana in terms of politics versus antipolitics. These narcotics, too, are merely salable materials, except that, if used beyond prudence, they can be quite disabling to the person using them. (I inject that note simply because, in my understanding, there remains at all levels of addiction the chance of breaking or controlling the habit. This suggests that the person *can* exercise a choice in the matter; that he can, indeed, be prudent or not.)

The person who uses drugs imprudently, just as the person who imprudently uses the politically sanctioned and franchised drugs of alcohol or tobacco, ends up in an unenviable position, perhaps dead. That, rationally, is his own business, as long as he does not, by his action, deprive you of the right to make your own decision not to use drugs, to assist addicts, or, if you wish, to ignore them. But it is said, by right and left today, that the real problem is social and public—that the high price of the drugs leads the addict to rob and kill (rightist position), and that making drugs a public matter, for clinical dispensation, would eliminate the causes of his crime (leftist position).

These both are essentially political positions, and clearly inept in a society where the line between mind–expanders such as coffee or LSD is highly technical. By choosing the economic and cultural approach rather than a political one, the antipolitical libertarian would say, sell away. Competition will keep the price down. Cultural acceptance of the root ethic, that a man's life and its appurtenances are inviolate, would justify defense against any violence that might accompany addiction in others. And what is there left for the "public" to do? Absolutely nothing—except, individually, to decide whether to risk drugs or to avoid them. Parents, of course, holding the purse strings of their children, can exercise a certain amount of control, but only individually, never collectively.

Incidentally, it is easy to imagine that, if drugs were left to economics and culture instead of politics, medical researchers would shortly discover a way to provide the salable and wanted effects of drugs without the incapacitation of addiction. In this as in similar matters— such as the unregulated competition from which it is felt people need protection—technology rather than politics might offer far better answers.

Monopoly is a case in point. To suppose that anyone needs government protection from the creation of monopolies is to accept two suppositions: that monopoly is the natural direction of unregulated enterprise, and that technology is static. Neither, of course, is true. The great concentrations of economic power, which are called monopolies today, did not grow *despite* government's antimonopolistic zeal. They grew, largely, *because* of government policies, such as those making it more profitable for small businesses to sell out to big companies rather than fight the tax code alone. Additionally, federal fiscal and credit policies and federal subsidies and contracts have all provided substantially more assistance to big and established companies than to smaller, potentially competitive ones. The auto industry receives the biggest subsidy of all, through the highway program on which it prospers, but for which it surely does not pay a fair share. Airlines are subsidized and so protected that newcomers can't even try to compete. Television networks are fantastically advantaged by FCC licensing, which prevents upstarts from entering a field where big one–timers have been established. Even in agriculture, it is large and established farmers who get the big subsidies—not small ones who might want to compete. Government laws specifically exempting unions from antitrust activities have also furthered a monopoly mentality. And, of course, the "public utility" and "public transportation" concepts have specifically created government–licensed monopolies in the fields of power, communications, and transit. This is not to say that economic bigness is bad. It isn't, if it results from economic efficiency. But it is bad if it results from collusion with political rather than with economic power. There is no monopoly situation in the world today, of which I can think, that might not be seriously challenged by competition, were it not for some form of protective government license, tariff, subsidy, or regulation. Also, there isn't the tiniest shred of evidence to suggest that the trend of unregulated business and industry is toward monopoly. In fact, the trend seems in the opposite direction, toward diversification and decentralization.

The technological aspect is equally important. Monopoly cannot develop as long as technology is dynamic, which it most abundantly is today. No corporation is so large that it can command every available brain—except, of course, a corporate state. As long as one brain remains unavailable, there is the chance of innovation and competition. There can be no real monopoly, just momentary advantage. Nor does technological breakthrough always depend upon vast resources or, even where it does, would it have to depend upon a single source of financing—unless, again, only the state has the money. Short of total state control, and presuming there are creative brains in the community, and presuming the existence of capital with which to build even modest research facilities, few would flatly say that technological innovation could be prevented simply because of some single source enjoying a temporary "monopoly" of a given product or service. The exceptions, to repeat, are always governments. Governments can be—and usually are—monopolistic. For instance, it is not uneconomical to operate a private post–office department today. It is only illegal. The Feds enjoy a legal monopoly—to the extent that they are currently prosecuting at least one entrepreneur who operated a mail service better and cheaper than they do.

Politics is not needed to prevent monopoly. Unregulated, unrestricted laissez–faire capitalism is all that is needed. It would also provide jobs, raise living standards, improve products, and so forth. If commercial activity were unregulated and absolutely unsubsidized, it could depend upon only one factor for success: pleasing customers.

Censorship is another notable example in which politics, and politicians, interpose between customer and satisfaction. The gauge becomes not whether the customer is happy, but whether the politician (either singly or as a surrogate for "the public") is happy. This applies equally to "public" protection from unpopular political ideas as well as protection from pornography. Conservatives are at least consistent in this matter. They feel that the state (which they sometimes call "the community") can and must protect people from unsavory thoughts. It goes without saying who defines "unsavory": the political—or community—leaders, of course.

DOUBLE STANDARD

Perhaps the most ironic of all manifestations of this conservative urge to cleanthink concerns the late Lenny Bruce. He talked dirty. He was, therefore, a particularly favorite target of conservatives. He was also an explicit and, I think, incisive defender of capitalism. In commenting that communism is a drag ("like one big phone company"), Bruce specifically opted for capitalism ("it gives you a choice, baby, and that's what it's about"). There is no traditional conservative who is fit even to walk on the same level with Lenny Bruce in his fierce devotion to individualism. Lenny Bruce frequently used what is for many conservatives the dirtiest word of all: he said "capitalism." When was the last time that the N.A.M. did as much?

Lenny Bruce wasn't the only man to alienate conservatives by opening his mouth. In 1964, Barry Goldwater alienated southern conservatives in droves when, in answer to a regionally hot question about whether communists should be permitted to speak on state-university campuses, Goldwater said, flatly and simply: "Of course they should."

Even anticommunist libertarians have no choice but to deny the state the right to suppress communists. Similarly, libertarians who are aesthetically repelled by what they deem pornography have no other course than not to buy it, leaving its absolutely unregulated sale to producer, purchaser, and no one else. Once again, a parent could intrude—but only by stopping an individual, dependent purchaser, never by stopping the purveyor, whose right to sell pornography for profit, and for absolutely no other socially redeeming virtue whatever, would be inviolate. An irate parent who attempted to hustle a smut peddler off the street, as a matter of fact, should be sued, not saluted.

The liberal attitude toward censorship is not so clear. At this point, it needn't be. Liberals practice it, rather than preach it. The FCC's egregious power to insist that broadcasting serve a social purpose is both a liberal tenet and an act of censorship. In the FCC canons, social purposes are defined so that a station can get good points for permitting a preacher free time, but no points—or even bad points—for extending the same gift of free air time to an atheist.

It is partly in the realm of air, also, that differences regarding nationalism between the old left–right politicians and the libertarian anti–politician show up. If today's conservative has his fervent jingoism for old nations, the liberal has just as fanatic a devotion to the jingoism of new nations. The willingness of modern liberals to suggest armed intervention against South Africa, while ignoring, even in terms of major journalistic coverage, slaughters in Nigeria and the Sudan, is a demonstration of interest only in politics—and in particular persons—rather than in human life per se.

Of course, conservatives have a similar double standard in regard to anticommunist slaughter and anticommunist dictatorship. Although it is not as whimsically selective as the liberal decision to be revolted or cheered by each particular blood bath, the conservative double standard can have equally tragic results. The distinct undercurrents of anti–Semitism that so obviously muddle many conservative movements probably can be traced to the horrid assumption that Adolf Hitler's anticommunism excused his other, but comparatively minor, faults. Somehow, anticommunism seems to permit anti–Semitism.

I have met in my time many anticommunists who view communism as simply a creature of Jewish plotting for world dominion. The John Birch Society's separate chapter for Jewish members is a seriocomic reflection, I think, of such good old WASP anti–Semitism. The widely reported admiration of Hitler by the head man of the right–wing Liberty Lobby is a reflection, presumably, of the "you need a strong man to fight atheistic communism" school of thought. There are, of course, notable Jewish anticommunists. And there are many anticommunists who condemn anti–Semitism. But the operating question for most of the full-time anticommunists that I have met is simply: are you anticommunist? Being also anti–Semitic is not automatically a disqualification on the right, though it usually is on the left.

Conservatives and liberals alike hold in common the mystical notion that nations really mean something, probably something permanent. Both ascribe to lines drawn on maps—or in the dirt or in the air—the magical creation of communities of men that require sovereignty and sanction. The conservative feels this with exaltation when he beholds the Stars and Stripes. The liberal feels this with academic certitude when he concludes that Soviet boundaries must be "guaranteed" to prevent Soviet nervousness. Today, in the ultimate confusion, there are people who feel that the lines drawn by the Soviet Union, in blood, are better than the lines drawn, also in blood, by American foreign policy. Politicians just think this way.

The radical and revolutionary view of the future of nationhood is, logically, that it has no future, only a past— often an exciting one, and usually a historically useful one at some stage. But lines drawn on paper, on the ground, or in the stratosphere are clearly insufficient to the future of mankind.

Again, it is technology that makes it feasible to con-template a day in which the politics of nationhood will be as dead as the politics of power–wielding partisanship. First, there is enough information and wealth available to ensure the feeding of all people, without the slaughtering of some to get at the possessions of others. Second, there is no longer any way to protect anything or anybody behind a national boundary anyway.

Not even the Soviet Union, with what conservatives continue to fear as an "absolute" control over its people, has been able to stop, by drawing lines or executing thousands, the infusion of subversive ideas, manners, music, poems, dances, products, desires. If the world's preeminent police state (either we or they, depending upon your *political* point of view) has been unable to protect itself fully behind its boundaries, what faith can or should we, the people, retain in boundaries?

It is to be expected that both liberals and conservatives respond to the notion of the end of nationhood with very similar shouts of outrage or jerks of reaction. The conservative says *it shall not be.* There will always be a U.S. Customs Inspector and long may he wave. The liberal says that far from ending nationhood, he wants to expand it, make it worldwide, to create a proliferation of mini– and macro–nations in the name of ethnic and cultural preservation, and then to erect a great super-bureaucracy to supervise all the petty bureaucracies.

Like Linus, neither liberal nor conservative can bear the thought of giving up the blanket—giving up government and going it alone as residents of a planet, rather than of a country. Advocates of isolationism (although some, admittedly, defend it only as a tactic) seem to fall into a paradox here. Isolationism not only depends upon nationhood, it rigidifies it. There is a subcategory of isolationism, however, that might avoid this, by specifying that it favors only military isolationism, or the use of force only for self–defense. Even this, however, requires political definitions of self–defense in these days of missiles, bases, bombers, and subversion.

As long as there are governments powerful enough to maintain national boundaries and national political postures, there will be the absolute risk, if not the certainty, of war between them. Even the possibility of war seems far too cataclysmic to contemplate in a world so ripe with technology and prosperous potential, ripe even with the seeds of extraterrestrial exploration. Violence and the institutions that alone can support it should be rendered obsolete.

POWER OF DEATH

Governments wage war. The power of life that they may claim in running hospitals or feeding the poor is just the mirror image of the power of death that they also claim—in filling those hospitals with wounded and in devastating lands on which food could be grown. "But man is aggressive," the right and left chant from the depths of their pessimism. To be sure, he is. But if he were left alone, if he were not regulated into states or services, wouldn't that aggression be directed toward conquering his environment, and not other men?

At another warlike level, it is the choice of aggression, against a politically perpetuated environment more than against men, that marks the racial strife in America today. Conservatives, in one of their favorite lapses of logic—states' rights—nourished modern American racism by supporting laws, particularly in southern states, that gave the state the power to force businessmen to build segregated facilities. (Many businesses, to be sure, wanted to be "forced," thus giving their racism the seal of state approval.) The states' rights lapse is simply that conservatives who deny to the federal government certain controls over people, eagerly cede exactly the same controls to smaller administrative units. They say that the smaller units are more effective. This means that conservatives support the coercion of individuals at the most effective level. It certainly doesn't mean that they oppose coercion. In failing to resist state segregation and miscegenation laws, in failing to resist laws maintaining racially inequitable spending of tax money, simply because these laws were passed by states, conservatives have failed to fight the very bureaucracy that they supposedly hate—at the very level where they might have stopped it first.

Racism has been supported in this country not in spite of, but thanks to, governmental power and politics. Reverse racism, thinking that government is competent to force people to integrate, just as it once forced them to segregate, is just as political and just as disastrous. It has not worked.

Its product has been hatred rather than brotherhood.
Brotherhood could never be a political product. It is purely
personal. In racial matters, as in all other matters
concerning individuals, the lack of government would be
nothing but beneficial. What, actually, can government do
for black people in America that black people could not do
better for themselves, if they were permitted the freedom to
do so? I can think of nothing.

Jobs? Politically and governmentally franchised unions
do more to keep black men from good jobs than do all the
Bull Connors of the South. Homes, schools, and protection?
I recall very vividly a comment on this subject by Roy Innis,
since 1968 the National Chairman of the Congress of Racial
Equality (CORE). He spoke of Mayor John Lindsay's
typically liberal zeal in giving money to black people,
smothering them with it—or silencing them. Innis then said
that the one thing Mayor Lindsay (New York City, 1966–
1973) would not give the blacks was what they really
wanted: political power. He meant that the black
community in Harlem, for instance, rather than being gifted
with tax money by the bushel, would prefer to be gifted with
Harlem itself. It is a community. Why shouldn't it govern
itself, or at least live by itself, without having to be a barony
of New York City ward politics? However, I take exception to
the notion of merely building in Harlem a political structure
similar to but only separate from New York City's. And I
may be doing Mr. Innis, who is an exceptional man, an
injustice by even suggesting that that is what he had in
mind.

But beyond this one instance, there is implicit in the
very exciting undercurrent of black power in this country an
equally exciting possibility that it will develop into a
rebellion against politics itself. It might insist upon a far
less structured community, containing far more voluntary
institutions within it. There is no question in my mind that,
in the long run, this movement and similar ones will
discover that *laissez–faire* is the way to create genuine
communities of voluntarism. Laissez–faire is the only form
of social–economic organization that could tolerate and even
bless a kibbutz operating in the middle of Harlem, a hippie
selling hashish down the street, and a few blocks farther
on, a firm of engineers out to do in Detroit with a low–cost

nuclear vehicle.

The kibbutz would represent, in effect, a voluntary socialism—what other form could free men tolerate? The hash seller would represent institutionalized—but voluntary—daydreaming, and the engineers would represent unregulated creativity. All would represent laissez–faire capitalism in action, and none would need a political officeholder or a single bureaucrat to help, hinder, civilize, or stimulate. And, in the process simply of variegated existence, the residents of this voluntary community, as long as others voluntarily entered into commerce with them, would solve the "urban" problem in the only way it ever can be solved; *i.e.*, via the vanishment of politics that created the problem in the first place.

If cities cannot exist on the basis of the skills, energy, and creativity of the people who live, work, or invest in them, then they should not be sustained by people who do *not* live in them. In short, every community should be one of voluntarism, to the extent that it lives for and through its own people, and does not force others to pay its bills. Communities should not be exempted from the civil liberty prescribed for people—the exclusive employment of all their own powers for their own welfare. This means that no one should serve you involuntarily, and that you should not involuntarily serve anyone else. For communities, this means existing without involuntary aid from other communities, or to other communities.

Student dissenters today seem to feel that somehow they crashed through to new truths and new politics in their demands that universities and communities be made responsive to their students or inhabitants. But most of them are only playing with old politics. When the dissenters recognize this, and when their assault becomes one against political power and authority rather than a fight to gain such power, then this movement may release the bright potential latent in the intelligence of so many of its participants. Incidentally, to the extent that student activists the world over are actually fighting the existence of political power, rather than trying to grab some of it for themselves, they should not be criticized for failing to offer alternative programs; *i.e.*, for not spelling out just what sort of political system will follow their revolution. What ought to follow their revolution is just what they've implicitly proposed: no political system at all.

The style of SDS (Students for a Democratic Society) so far seems most promising in this respect. It is itself loosely knit and internally anti–authoritarian, as well as externally revolutionary. Liberty also looks for students who, rather than caterwauling the establishment, will abandon it, establish their own schools, make them effective, and who will wage a concerned and concerted revolt against the political regulations and power that, today, give a franchise to schools—public and private—that badly need competition from new schools with new ideas.

Looking back, this same sort of thinking was true during the period of the sit–ins in the South. Since the enemy was state laws requiring separate facilities, why wasn't it also a proper tactic to defy such laws by building a desegregated eating place and holding it against hell and high water? This is a cause to which any libertarian could respond.

Similarly with the school situation. Find someone who will rebel against public–education laws and you will have a worthy rebel indeed. Find someone who just rants in favor of getting more liberals, or more conservatives, onto the school board, and you will have found a politically oriented, passé man—a plastic rebel. Or, in the blackest neighborhood, find the plumber who will thumb his nose at City Hall's restrictive licenses and certificates and you will have found a freedom fighter of far greater consequence than the window-breaker.

Power and authority, as substitutes for performance and rational thought, are the specters that haunt the world today. They are the ghosts of awed and superstitious yesterdays. And politics is their familiar. Politics, throughout time, has been an institutionalized denial of man's ability to survive through the exclusive employment of all his own powers for his own welfare. And politics, throughout time, has existed solely through the resources that it has been able to plunder from the creative and productive people whom it has, in the name of many causes and moralities, denied the exclusive employment of all their own powers for their own welfare.

Ultimately, this must mean that politics denies the rational nature of man. Ultimately, it means that politics is just another form of residual magic in our culture—a belief that somehow things come from nothing, that things may be given to some without first taking them from others, that all the tools of man's survival are his by accident or divine right, and not by pure and simple inventiveness and work.

Politics has always been the institutionalized and established way in which some men have exercised the power to live off the output of other men. But even in a world made docile to these demands, men do not need to live by devouring other men.

Politics does devour men. A laissez–faire world would liberate men. And it is in that sort of liberation that the most profound revolution of all may be just beginning to stir. It will not happen overnight, just as the lamps of rationalism were not quickly lighted and have not yet burned brightly. But it will happen—because it must happen. Man can survive in an inclement universe only through the use of his mind. His thumbs, his nails, his muscles, and his mysticism will not be enough to keep him alive without it.

This essay came from Hess's award–winning 1969 *Playboy* article by the same title. A one-time speechwriter for Senator Barry Goldwater, Karl Hess (1923–1994) worked in the news media, becoming an editor at *Newsweek*. Considered an anarcho–capitalist writer, Hess co-founded *Left and Right: A Journal of Libertarian Thought,* with Professor Murray Rothbard in 1965. During the 1960's, he was critical of big business, big government, and the military–industrial complex, and joined Students for a Democratic Society (SDS) to protest the Vietnam war. In later years, he became active in the Libertarian Party, and from 1986 to 1990, edited its national newspaper. He authored nine books, including *Dear America* (1975) and *Community Technology* (1979).

CHAPTER 5

MORAL LAW

By Robert LeFevre

Is there a moral law? Do such things as moral principles exist?

For centuries, scholars and philosophers have concluded that morality is a derivative of custom, and nothing more. Since customs vary from tribe to tribe, clime to clime, and nation to nation, it has seemed impossible to establish a single criterion of "good" and "bad" which would be worldwide in application and acceptance.

What is "good" in one location at a given period may be viewed as neutral, or possibly even "bad," at the same time in some other location. Further, conceptions of the "good" do not remain constant even in a single location. Although standards of what is moral and what is immoral tend to have long lives because they are absorbed by each new generation, and become the ethos and the mores of each distinct grouping, there are gradual developments which bring shadings of interpretation, and even sharp alteration in direction.

In short, the realm of morals has been subjective.

"Good" and "bad" are matters of opinion; and while we all have opinions about how people "ought" to behave, no central, objective evidence has been accepted so as to assure unanimity of view. Perhaps Mark Twain summed it up when he declared, "nothing needs reform so much as other people's morals."

It is the purpose of this writing to establish that a moral law does exist. This means that I intend to show by the use of scientific methodology—by employing reason and logic— that an objective position can be found which could be universally accepted, and cannot honestly be denied by anyone willing to employ the same tools.

Unfortunately, in entering this area of discussion, the landscape is difficult to discern, because it has been fogged in by various religious and theological arguments. I seek neither to refute nor confirm any religious or theological view. That is grist for another mill. Atheist, deist, theist, agnostic, and polytheist should be comfortable, for I propose to examine the moral issue in an entirely secular and lay fashion. I am looking for something that exists in the nature of things as they are, which, if properly examined, will establish that there is in such existing phenomena a discernible rule of logic telling human beings what they ought to do; or, more precisely, telling them what they ought not to do. I am looking for a natural law.

A natural law can be discovered whenever a limited number of known factors are put together in a specific way, so that the reaction from that placement produces constant and consistent reaction in a predictable manner. All natural laws are discovered; human beings do not create them. The discovery is confirmed when known factors (A–B–C) are put together under specific conditions (X), and a predictable outcome (Y) always ensues.

When A–B–C are joined under specific conditions, but Y manifests only 70 percent of the time, then we have not made the discovery of a principle; rather, we have discovered a probability. One can have respect for a probability, but one is compelled by reality to accept a principle. All true principles are manifestations of nature, or, if you prefer, manifestations of the nature of reality. In short, things react according to what they are. When we learn what they are, then we can predict how they will react.

Bear in mind that all knowledge, whether it leads to probability or principle, is found in context. The conditions under which known factors are examined are at least as important as any of the factors themselves. Thus, we might say that the nature of wood is such that it can be used readily as a fuel—in context, of course. Some wood, if submerged in water over an extensive time, becomes waterlogged, and under ordinary conditions will not burn. So the principle that wood predictably can be used as a fuel is modified by nature and the condition of the wood at the time. Burning anything requires oxygen. Put flammable wood into all the appropriate contextual factors, but remove the oxygen, and the wood will not burn. Again, predictability is modified—this time by the possible omission of a contextual factor.

Thus, in a sense, all human knowledge contains a possible flaw.

With our limited human comprehension, we do not know all the contextual factors that might exist in the universe. With a limited time span in which to learn, and with virtually no awareness whatever of what might exist in remote portions of a universe impossible for us to sense, anything we presently know could be modified by something we might later discover.

To illustrate, I have heard many students argue that Newton's Law of Gravity was disproved by Einstein's theories. The fact is that Einstein did not dispute Newton's findings. Newton's findings still stand in context. Einstein enlarged the context to introduce factors not yet considered. Thanks to Newton and the predictability of the Law of Gravity (in context) we have an aviation industry, a building industry, and many other industries which function in the context of our daily lives at the present time. These industries exist because the law of gravity works precisely as Newton said it did; the Law of Gravity has not been repealed.

Returning to the question of morality, it is significant that nature, qua nature, provides us humans with no visible evidence of cause and effect respecting our own view of the "good" and the "bad." The overarching view of religion has probably served to influence thinking and research in this area. What savants and scholars have sought to find was something in nature which would react to man's "immoral" (i.e., unacceptable) behavior.

Here is a man who spends his life cheating, stealing, and robbing others. Is there something in nature which decrees that sooner or later he will suffer for these negative and unwanted actions? Studies indicate that there is no natural retaliation. While it may be true that some thieves will suffer, it is equally true that some will not. The miscreant must protect himself from his outraged neighbors who know of his excesses, but the rain and the sun treat him the same way they treat others. All the laws of nature behave toward the thief exactly as they behave toward his victims.

Throughout nature, it is the fit who survive. The big fish eats the little fish, if the big fish is capable. There is zero indication that nature frowns upon the big fish. Nature seems to ask only one question: "Can you survive?" It does not ask: "Should you survive?"

While some have argued that misdeeds will be punished in some other life, if not in this one, the very growth and dominance of governments furnish evidence that most people don't believe this argument. Few believe that justice which misfired during life will somehow hit the mark after death. The man of faith believes that justice will come at the hands of God, but those who lack that faith, sue. They want justice here and now, because they aren't certain any will be forthcoming later on.

In view of these findings, which are common to us all, how can one postulate the existence of a "law" of moral behavior? Nature does not punish evildoers, and appears neutral only to effective survivors. Nature has no time for ineptitude.

In considering the context in which moral questions are discussed, I propose to introduce a contextual factor that until now has been omitted. Since we have grown accustomed to discovering principles only in respect to tangible phenomena, our approach to morality has been along that line. But morality does not relate to anything tangible, and cannot be found in a world consisting of tangible things. Morality is a concept about how we would like other people to behave. Therefore, morality is an idea. This means that it is a derivative of the mind and, hence, is subjective.

Heretofore, we have deduced all principles from the behavior of objective phenomena. Now, we must seek to find a principle in an arena wherein it has long been accepted that objective findings are impossible to deduce.

The contextual factor, which has been overlooked, relates to a particular way of looking at man qua man. Insensibly, most scholars have treated the genus Homo as something apart from nature. Man is viewed as having an impact (usually negative) upon the "natural" world. Few have taken the time to learn that man is neither contra-natural nor anti-natural. Man is as much a part of nature as anything else in the universe. Man is simply a species of living creatures made of the stuff which is found in the universe; and, as far as is known, is incapable of ever leaving the universe. Man's impact upon nature, while impressive and profound, is no more hostile to nature than any other phenomenon of nature acting within a natural universe.

If we begin to recognize man as co–existent with and part of the natural order, we will have to accept that the brains with which mankind is endowed are also part of the natural order. This means that the "mindset" human beings acquire as a result of experience and learning is the natural product of the natural brains of natural beings. Man is, it seems, more a creature of this world, this solar system, and this galaxy within the universe than he cares to believe.

Looking at our particular species as part of nature opens the door to the possibility that predictability may exist within the mental arena when we are dealing only with concepts, and when everything of which we speak is subjective.

Since human brains are natural, and the mind–set of any given individual is a result of this accumulation of data, attitude, and desire, as well as his reaction to the nature of the universe and the stuff of which the universe is made, it would follow that instead of seeking amid tangible phenomena for objective cause and effect, we should seek within context, or within the conceptual arena, for predictability.

This means that if we could create the conditions of a mental experiment, we could discover whether a single viewpoint emerges. If we could observe a mental reaction to a particular set of circumstances under controlled conditions (in context), and in consequence find that without exception, every human mind will take this position, then we would have found a principle where it has been thought that none could be found. Predictability in the world of ideas should be as acceptable as predictability in the world of tangible objects (in context).

Since we here are discussing only one thing, moral law, I

will largely omit discussion of the nature of man and the nature of human property, examination of both of which would otherwise be germane at this juncture. I am omitting them by presuming that the reader has a working knowledge of his own nature and of the role property plays in his own life.

I must, however, make one point. In man's long struggle emerging from a primordial, prehistoric beginning, it is only those who own property who have been concerned about the behavior of others in a moral sense. Before property ideas were developed, humans lived in small groups as hunters and foragers. In the ensuing hand–to–mouth economy, owning property had virtually no meaning. The single item of transcendent value was food, always in short supply. When food was found, it was probably eaten at once.

As the species developed its intellectual powers, and began to devise tools and to learn, among other things, that some land is more advantageous than other land, obtaining and keeping control of its land, its water supply, and its food sources became factors of primary concern. The amoral view of the hunter and forager (you can eat anything you can grab) was gradually replaced by a taboo: It is wrong to eat (take) something that someone else has grabbed ahead of you, but from which he hasn't yet reaped all the good that he wants.

Thus, concern about how other people behave initially emerged from the wishes of property owners, not from the wishes of those who did not own. This situation continues today. Those with little or nothing have no difficulty in rationalizing theft as a beneficial act if, as a result of theft, the have–nots become (even momentarily) "haves."

But a fascinating change in attitude occurs abruptly in the minds of any persons who benefit from theft. When they see themselves as a "have" in a given area, they are highly incensed if a suggestion is made that anyone has a moral prerogative to steal from them. Few are more hostile to theft than those who have benefited only recently from it, and fear a reaction. They don't mind stealing from others. The "others" can always manage, but they are outraged if the sticky fingers of kleptomania reach into their own pockets.

What can be seen readily is that it is natural for human

beings to seek to protect whatever belongs to them. Whether it is their life or their fortune, whatever is owned is precious.

What must be underscored is this: the emergence of man from a primitive life, described by Hobbes as "nasty, brutish and short," is the result of man's yearning to be safe and unmolested in what he owns. If societal relations could exist in a group of humans who own properties in varying amounts, but who, despite greed and envy, refrain from stealing, then a moral society would exist.

The function of this essay, however, has nothing to do with the various methods which have been tried in an effort to eliminate or at least to minimize theft. Rather, the attempt is being made to show that the moral "law" alluded to can be discerned by scientific methods and by the use of logic and reason. Before seeking to offer a single set of opinions to anyone about anything, it sure would be desirable to show that any conclusions being offered are in harmony with reality (within our present range of knowledge), and that they comply with the criteria of careful and precise thought.

However, we can make an interim summary. Moral ideas are related to ideas respecting the ownership of property. My personal view has it that property owners, invariably the beneficiaries of any effective system against theft, are the originators of moral concepts; but I do not know that in any scientific way. Based on what I do know, it seems most likely; however, there can be no question that a relationship between ownership and moral ideas exists as an historic fact, even if other unconfirmed factors exist.

Let us return to the central theme. Every item of property, as well as every person, exists within its own exterior limits. This is to say, that every property and every person has a discernible physical boundary. If the boundary is not readily discernible (as with parcels of land, odors, sounds, broadcast frequencies, ideas, etc.), human language is such that it can be used to locate and fix such boundaries.

In view of this fact, we may recognize that each human being owns (and controls) himself (his own person), and that all other properties he owns, and/or controls in whole or in part, will be treated by that person as extensions of himself. Regardless of the amount or kind of property involved, every human being will predictably object to a trespass of any of his physical boundaries, if such trespass occurs without his consent. Stated another way, no human being will approve of his own victimization. The victimization can be against his person or against something he owns—as in cases of theft, arson, embezzlement, etc.—but the victim will predictably disapprove.

Various notions as to what property is, and how it is to be owned or possessed, exist in various places in the world, but these variables do not affect the outcome. To the degree that an individual accepts the ownership of himself by himself, to the degree that he believes he is the owner of something beyond his own person, to that degree, he will resent the violation of his property boundary.

To be precise, the predictable reaction of every human intelligence could be phrased as a rejection of the assumption of power over his own decision–making faculty and ability, by another specimen of his own kind.

It might be true, and frequently is true, that interference by parents with their children's decision–making ability might be beneficial, even to the point of saving lives. This doesn't really matter to a child; he resents the intrusion, preferring to make his own decisions regardless. A violation of his will in this regard may induce all manner of violent reaction until he manages to gain some degree of control.

Because of this, I am not seeking to predict what a given individual will do as a result of a boundary violation. This may well depend upon his ability to restrain himself in the face of provocation. What can be predicted is that the individual whose boundaries are trespassed will resent it, regardless of what he does in response.

It is important to stress that this discovery of predictability does not claim that all human beings resent each and every property violation. That is decidedly not the case. In many instances, human beings will be eager for a property boundary violation and will clamor for it. Bear in mind that the finding of which I speak arises only in context. The very individual who will cry loudly for intervention across his neighbor's boundaries, will resent and disapprove of similar intervention if his own boundaries are involved.

No human being wishes to be victimized. If and when victimization has occurred, it is logical and reasonable to assume (regardless of how he may react) that he disapproved.

It is my belief that all discussions respecting "crime" have arisen over this question of boundary violation. We have discovered that in prehistory men were already engaged in nefarious behavior which involved property trespasses against whole groups or against individuals.

Concepts of "good" and "bad" behavior are tied to these events. A "good" person committed no act of aggression against his neighbor's boundaries: a "bad" person did. Therefore, it was easy to discern that from the standpoint of any potential victim, moral (desirable) behavior would consist of non–trespass. This appears to hold true whether we are speaking of interpersonal or international relationships.

The ambivalence of human behavior is crystal clear. Those who view themselves as the victors and the profit-makers have no moral compunction about violating the boundaries of others. An extensive rationale exists: "They are rich and we are poor, so we must destroy the rich." "They deserve theft, because they are thieves, too." "They might hurt us, so let us hurt them first." "They are different from us, and we don't understand them." "They are poor and want what we have, so we must protect ourselves from the poor." And on and on.

Those who have been victimized by aggressors and anticipate that it could happen again, are far less certain of the merit of theft. Rather, they at last begin to make an appeal on moral grounds. Unhappily they often make objections to "this particular" boundary violation, but reserve the privilege of approving of other violations. A solid opposition to boundary violation on principle is more effective than piecemeal objection, or complaints that one particular type of weapon is horrible, "inhumane," or "uncalled for."

But the persons favoring bellicosity refer to moral arguments as "cowardly" or "helpful to our enemy" (when they decide which boundary is target for today's aggression). The result is in the nature of a stalemate, with efforts to identify a moral law almost abandoned.

Personally, I believe that the moral position, derived logically and employing the scientific method (i.e., limited factors, controlled conditions, predictable results) is mandatory. To show that, I must take one more step.

True morality cannot be discerned merely by virtue of a universal mindset based on predictability. It could provide us with a unanimity of what people have found desirable, but it must do more than that.

A moral position must be consonant in fact with the real nature of our species. And the fact is that antipathy against property boundary violation must be based on what is objectively in harmony with the real world; not merely subjectively desirable.

Man is capable of experiencing both pain and pleasure. It is a small step to recognize that pain inflicted by one person upon another is universally unwelcome. Even the masochist, who enjoys certain types of pain, does not welcome it when it is imposed upon him. Inflicted pain is, therefore, contrary to the real nature of man, and counterproductive to his best interests.

But is a property boundary violation inherently painful?

Granting that damage inflicted physically on a person's body induces pain, is damage inflicted upon something that person owns always painful? Bear in mind that the principle I am setting forth makes no such claim. It is not the damage itself (e.g., theft, arson, vandalism) that is the definitive pain factor, but rather the violation of the will of that property's owner, in respect to that property. The violation of a person's will to control what is his is universally painful.

Although I have conceded that in cases involving children, parental intervention across boundaries may prove beneficial and even necessary, this is only a temporary condition. Were parental intervention to continue too long, the child would be overprotected to his ultimate detriment. Crossing the boundary of a child, when absolutely essential, should be viewed as a form of punishment and used sparingly, only for the purpose of instruction. In terms of man qua man, violating the boundaries of others, even if you are smarter, bigger, richer, and more experienced than your victim, is counterproductive to his ultimate development as well as your own.

Intervention in the lives and properties of others against their wills, "for their own good," tends to make them dependent upon you—a doubly counterproductive consequence.

What is truly important to grasp is that in speaking of morality, I have not meant to imply that nature or nature's God deplores bad conduct and reacts to punish the offender. The indifference of nature is compensated for by the enormous concern of owners within our own species.

Let me summarize the moral law as the evidence shows: violating the boundary of person, or property of any human being, against the wishes of that person, is a wrongful act and is counterproductive to the general well-being of humankind.

Any violation of the moral law consists of an error in judgment.

Every crime that occurs—that is, every violation of a boundary, for there is no such thing as a real crime that does not entail a boundary violation—is a mistake in judgment on the part of a human being.

Mankind, being human, will make mistakes in judgment. Some errors are more serious than others, but in the end, were we clever enough and well enough informed, it is conceivable that we could create a moral society in which no one ever violated the boundary of another. It is conceivable. That is to say, it is a concept I can visualize.

For it to actualize, for it to come about as an objective reality, the development of the human mind would have to be so complete at such an early date, that even children would "listen to reason," and intervention across their boundaries would never be necessary or desirable.

I trust you will pardon my skepticism. Given the nature of our species as it presently exists, I profoundly doubt the creation of such a society.

Despite this doubt, I am profoundly excited about moral law as I have stated it. I have found it not only possible, but relatively easy to live my life according to that moral law. I haven't done it perfectly, but I have managed to upgrade my performance. If I can make that claim even in the face of those who have known me for many years, then certainly it would be possible for anyone else to follow the same set of tenets and, in consequence, have the satisfaction I have reaped by so doing.

Robert LeFevre (1911–1986) founded Rampart College in 1957 in Colorado Springs, Colorado. Among the many notable teachers at his school were Milton Friedman, F.A. Harper, Leonard Read, Ludwig von Mises, and Rose Wilder Lane. Often viewed as a pacifist, LeFevre, who was a radio personality and writer, influenced a whole generation of libertarian thinkers. He authored many books, including *The Nature of Man and his Government* and *The Fundamentals of Liberty*. One of his quotes became legendary: "If men are good, you don't need government; if men are evil or ambivalent, you don't dare have one."

CHAPTER 6

THE PROTOCOLS OF THE LEARNED EXPERTS ON HEROIN

By Thomas Szasz, M.D.

The children of each generation are taught to want what they are taught they must not have.

– R. G. Collingwood, 1939

Why did the forgery of Janet Cooke's ugly story about an "8-Year-Old Heroin Addict (Who) Lives for a Fix" go undetected at *The Washington Post*? Why did she win a Pulitzer Prize? Although these are two unrelated questions, the same answer fits both. I believe that this fabrication went undetected and won a Pulitzer Prize because it purported to prove, once more, that heroin is our deadliest enemy.

Religious and medical propaganda notwithstanding, I hold some simple truths to be self-evident. One of these truths is that just as the dead do not rise from the grave, so drugs do not commit crimes. The dead remain dead, and drugs are inert chemicals that have no effect on human beings who choose not to use them. No one has to smoke cigarettes, and no one has to shoot heroin. People smoke cigarettes because they want to, and they shoot heroin because they want to. Furthermore, so far as the connection between heroin and crime is concerned, I contend that, the propaganda of the anti–drug crusader to the contrary notwithstanding, this truth is also self–evident: people under the influence of a drug that is a powerful central nervous system depressant, such as heroin, are less likely, rather than more likely, to commit crimes, than are those not under the influence of such a drug. On the other hand, people living in a society in which the use of certain drugs is popular, in which the sale of those drugs is prohibited, and in which the drug prohibitions are not enforced, are indeed more likely to commit crimes than they would be in the absence of those conditions. However, since no one is so blind as the man who does not want to see, these truths are quite powerless against popular mythologies, as *The New York Times'* editorial comment on the Cooke affair illustrates. Under the title "The Pulitzer Lie" (April 17, 1981), the editors of the *Times* emphasize their puzzlement:

> We do not know what possessed Janet Cooke to invent an interview with an imaginary 8–year–old drug addict who aspired to grow up to be a heroin pusher in the nation's capital. Nor do we know why *The Washington Post* was so quick to claim the protection of the First Amendment when city authorities sought help in locating children so obviously needing help. We do not know why this contested tale was then pushed for journalism's highest honor or why the Pulitzer Prize judges jumped the entry from one category to bestow the award.

Although I do not want to sound (or be) arrogant, I believe that I know the answer to these questions. Indeed, I believe that the editors of the *Times* know it too, albeit they do not want to admit it, or, as Freud has put it, they repress it. And the repressed, as Freud observed, invariably returns.

In this case, the repressed appears in another editorial only a few inches above "the Pulitzer Lie." In that comment, entitled "To Fight Crime, Fight Drugs," the editors admonish the Reagan administration for its insufficient zeal in fighting the drug menace. "The East Coast is currently swamped with heroin," we are informed. "In New York, drug–related robberies and burglaries have more than doubled in three years." But I am afraid that just as Janet Cooke's story about "Jimmy" was not true, so *The New York Times'* editorial about "drug–related crimes" is also not true. The crimes in question are not "drug–related" but "drug prohibition–related," which is not the same thing.

It is sad how quickly people have forgotten that when Nelson Rockefeller ran for Governor, his principal campaign strategy consisted of placing full–page advertisements in the newspapers showing the arm of a young black male injecting heroin. In the accompanying caption, Rockefeller pledged to free the people of New York State from this "plague" and the crime it "causes."

People seem also to have forgotten that Governor Hugh Carey offered this "truth" to explain why so many thugs stole so many gold chains in New York City. "The epidemic of gold–chain snatching in the city," declared Carey, "is the result of a Russian design to wreck America by flooding the nation with deadly heroin." "If the Russians were using nerve gas on us," the governor continued, "we'd certainly call out the troops. This is more insidious than nerve gas. Nerve gas passes off. This doesn't. It kills. I'm not overstating the case."

IN LOVE AND WAR

In love and war, all is supposed to be fair. The love of saving people from the Devil and the war on Evil have indeed always been regarded as ample justification for fabricating strategic lies. Let us face it: Cooke's story was *not* a "weird and atypical hoax," as the *Post* characterized it in hindsight. On the contrary, it was typical anti–drug propaganda, virtually indistinguishable from the standard pharmacomythological tales with which "professionals" and the media have been deluging the American public. If Cooke's story had been "weird and atypical," the editors of the *Post* would have displayed more skepticism toward it and the Pulitzer Prize judges would not have gone out of their way to honor it.

The adjective invariably used to describe the images that Cooke evoked is "shocking." Were a reporter to paint a similarly shocking picture today about, say, Jews poisoning wells, or black men raping white women, no respectable newspaper would print the story, nor would it win any prizes. That Janet Cooke's concoction was published, and that it won the coveted Pulitzer Prize, thus signify that she tapped a vital artery in America's body politic, a vessel nourishing our most sacred fears and prejudices. There is much evidence to support this view.

First, we have learned that, at the Pulitzer Prize board, one of the most enthusiastic defenders of Cooke's article was an editor from the *Washington Star* who, according to the *Times,* maintained that the piece deserved the prize because it "had done a great service," by alerting Washington residents to the problems of juvenile drug addiction. Then, there is the reaction of *Post* readers to Cooke's story, and reaction of *Post* staffers to it, both before and after its exposure as a fabrication. According to *Time* magazine, the editors at the *Post* "were comforted by letters from readers who claimed they knew Jimmy or children like him." At the *Post,* City Editor Milton Coleman was "very frankly surprised" that the police had not located Jimmy, and was so impressed by the piece that "he wanted another story on young addicts."

After the hoax was exposed, *Post* Executive Editor Benjamin Bradlee revealed that the *Post* can dish it out better than it can take it. In an ironic inversion of the Watergate scenario, in a front-page interview in the *Detroit Free Press,* Bradlee incriminated himself by "obstructing" not justice (since no crime had been committed), but what may be even more important, truth (since a lie had been published). When asked, "Have you talked to Cooke recently? What happened to her?" Bradlee replied:

> Well, I talked to her mother and father, but I haven't talked to her since early this morning. We're going to take care of her. We're going to see that she has professional help. We've talked to professional help about her, and we're going to get it for her and pay for it.

But Janet Cooke is neither a child nor an incompetent mental patient. Why talk to her parents? Why talk to "professional help"? Why call psychiatrists "professional help"? Why pay for the psychiatric treatment of a former *Post* employee who "resigns" to avoid being fired? I object to Bradlee's imposing an "insanity plea" on Cooke. Janet Cooke is a liar, not a lunatic, and Bradlee's casual categorization of her as a mental patient serves only to diminish further his own, and the *Post's* credibility.

More recently than most people care to admit, multitudes in the West celebrated their collective revulsion against what they then considered to be evil incarnate, the Jew, and its carrier, "International Zionism," through the mythopoesis of "The Protocols of the Learned Elders of Zion." Today, multitudes in the West celebrate their collective revulsion against what they now consider to be evil incarnate, heroin, and its carrier, the "pusher," through the mythopoesis of what could be called "The Protocols of the Learned Experts on Heroin." The Nazis did not have to invent new lies about Jews. Janet Cooke did not have to invent new lies about drugs.

The infamous "Protocols of the Learned Elders of Zion" was purported to be a true account of a conspiratorial plan for Jewish world conquest, drafted at a secret meeting of the first Zionist Congress in Basel, Switzerland, in 1897. The story was first published in the Russian newspaper *Znamia* ("The Banner") in 1903, and was quickly translated into German, French, English, and other western languages. The spurious character of this document was not revealed until 1921. Subsequently, it was established that the "Protocols" were commissioned by the Russian secret police. The full story of the forgery, as far as it could be uncovered, was not told until 1942.

We may not know it, or may not want to know it, but we live in an age in which we are deluged with a similar sort of allegedly true, but actually spurious, propaganda—about "drugs." One such example must suffice here.

Early in January, 1968, Raymond P. Shafer, then the Governor of Pennsylvania and subsequently the chairman of President Nixon's Marijuana Commission, announced to the press that six college students stared at the sun while under the influence of LSD, and as a result, were blinded.

The story was all over the country. Less than two weeks later, *The New York Times* reported that "The Governor, who yesterday told a news conference that he was convinced the report was true, said his investigators discovered this morning that the story was 'a fabrication' by Dr. Norman Yoder [Commissioner of the Office of the Blind].... He said Dr. Yoder, who was unavailable for comment, had admitted the hoax." What happened as a result of this disclosure? Nothing. Dr. Yoder and his lies were disposed of by the method characteristic of our age. Pennsylvania Attorney General William C. Sennet diagnosed Yoder as "sick," and attributed his fabrication to "his concern over illegal LSD use by children." Janet Cooke and the *Washington Post* were no doubt similarly concerned over heroin use by children.

At this point, it is necessary to focus on, and to expose, the key role that the imagery of helpless children—cared for by good people and corrupted by evil people—plays in the rhetoric of scapegoating. Gathering under this banner, the drug–mongers lost no time defending the morality of anti–heroin mendacity, even before the clamor over the nonexistent "Jimmy" had died down. For example, William Buckley (who really should know better), pleaded that we "go easy" on Janet Cooke, because "the story of an 8–year-old addicted to heroin is, in our wretched times, far from unlikely." No doubt, the idea of the menace of children as drug abusers seems "far from unlikely" to Buckley, just as the idea of the menace of children as self–abusers (masturbators) must have seemed far from unlikely to his father or grandfather. It is regrettable, however, that Buckley's boundless fear and loathing of heroin drives him to almost glorifying Janet Cooke, by comparing her well intentioned deception to the demonic deeds of the "pusher." "As one member of the white majority," writes Buckley, "I'd prefer the company of a black newspaperwoman who fabricated a story centered on a mythic *but entirely plausible little victim* [emphasis added] of drugs, to the company of the relatively untroubled black (or white) drug pushers who ride around in their Cadillacs sowing their poison."

But what has driving Cadillacs got to do with the morality of using heroin? Is murder more wicked if the killer leaves the scene in a Cadillac than if he leaves it on foot? If providing people with heroin is a grave wrong, as Mr. Buckley clearly believes it is, then giving it away gratis is at least as wicked as is selling it for a high price. In fact, Buckley is using cheap anti–capitalist rhetoric to whip up hatred against a scapegoat. Moreover, it is implicit in Buckley's argument that selling heroin is very bad, but selling cigarettes is not so bad, or not bad at all. Surely, it is unimaginable that Buckley would employ his anti–Cadillac rhetoric against the American tobacco barons and the "pushers" who distribute their toxic products.

Buckley's foregoing remarks articulate what is now considered to be the received truth about heroin. A lead letter in *The New York Times* by Don Russakoff—identified as the President of the Therapeutic Communities of America—illustrates further that the American "experts" know everything about "narcotics" that isn't so. Lamenting that the Cooke story proved to be false, Russakoff actually praises the *Post* for publishing it. "Tragically," he writes, "many other stories about pre–teen narcotic addicts never reach the front page, although they are indisputably true." But none of those stories is indisputably true. And even if they were, it would not follow—except as a leap of faith— that prohibiting the use of certain selected "dangerous drugs" is the correct social policy for dealing with the problem.

Revealingly, Russakoff, like Buckley, also bases his argument of a propagandistic use of the imagery of the child as drug victim. "Not long ago," he writes, "at one of our professional conferences, a physician described the case of a 6–year–old child who had "overdosed on 'angel dust.'" And what is that supposed to prove? That perhaps that physician, too, was a liar? That some parents neglect their children? That we should prohibit vacations in the Alps, lest children overdose on poisonous mushrooms,—or fall off the cliffs? Buckley and Russakoff are not presenting evidence or offering argument; they are whipping up mindless passion in the people against a scapegoat. Cooke may have written a false story, and the *Post* may have been misled into publishing it. But the Satanic threat remains, and the vigilance of the vigilantes is now more justified than ever, "The *Times, Washington Post,* and many other reasonable publications," concludes Russakoff, "have reported often on the worsening drug epidemic. It is real, not imaginary. And a high proportion of its victims are children. *Small children.*" (Emphasis added.)

As I suggested some time ago, the contemporary American attitude toward "dangerous drugs" is best understood in religious–mythological terms—that is, as the "ritual expulsion of evil" incarnated in a scapegoat. In the Yom Kippur ceremony, the scapegoat is a goat. In Christian anti-semitism, it is the Jew. In contemporary America, it is heroin (and the other illicit drugs). Once people accept something—an animal, a person, a people, a drug—as a scapegoat which incarnates Evil, they consider, *ipso facto*, the destruction of that scapegoat to be good. Consider, in this connection, the following:

• Formerly, Christians feared the Jews because, allegedly, they poisoned wells; accordingly, the Jews were savagely persecuted. Today, Americans fear heroin because, allegedly, it poisons people, especially young people; accordingly, heroin and heroin "pushers" are persecuted savagely. In fact, the Jews did not poison any wells, and heroin does not poison anyone. (The difficulty the contemporary reader has in seeing the difference between heroin poisoning someone and a person poisoning himself with heroin is a major symptom of the success of the anti-drug propaganda.)

• People who believe in a scapegoat do not want to understand it; they want to destroy it. When people regard Jews as Christ–killers or vermin, they do not want to understand Jews, they want a society free of Jews ("Judenfrei"). Similarly, when people regard heroin as a "killer drug" or as a worthless "poison," they do not want to understand heroin; they want a society free of heroin.

Perhaps deep in her soul Janet Cooke actually believed that "The Protocols of the Learned Experts on Heroin" were true, and perhaps she simply wanted to support their admonitory tale by adding to it a fresh chapter of her own. Let us not forget that, in the past, many devout persons had dramatic encounters with devils and saints, and no one called them liars; and that, in our own day, many "devout" persons have dramatic encounters with heroin pushers and cured addicts, and no one calls them liars. Janet Cooke told a rousing good tale, as a good writer should. She inflamed the public passion against the Enemy, as a good rhetorician is supposed to. To expect that her story should also be true—when hardly anyone else's story about "drugs" is true—seems almost unfair.

Concerning Janet Cooke's mythic hero, Jimmy, one more reflection is in order. Some people in Washington actually believed that they knew him. Cooke herself maintained, for as long as she could, that Jimmy was real. Obviously, there was virtually no way of proving that Jimmy did not exist. All of this made Cooke's denial or admission of the forgery exquisitely important. This leads to my final observation, namely, it seems quite possible that had Janet Cooke not lied about her academic credentials, her lies about heroin (for which the mythic Jimmy was, after all, only a vehicle) would probably have gone down America's collective gullet of gullibility just as smoothly as have all the other lies about heroin now passing as the received truth.

There is a moral to this story and it is this: no doubt unwittingly, Janet Cooke has done us a favor. She has held up a mirror in which we can catch a glimpse of a prevailing popular delusion. In the future, when people will worship at other shrines, they will scoff at our drug mythology, just as we now scoff at the blood and race mythologies of our fathers and grandfathers.

Will we ever learn one of history's more obvious lessons: to be especially on guard against those who lie to us by appealing to the welfare of children? How many Jews were murdered to save Christian children from being turned into matzo? The ritual murder of people has always been preceded by the ritual murder of the truth—and, indeed, by the ritual murder of language itself.

Dr. Thomas Szasz is Professor Emeritus in Psychiatry at the State University of New York Health Science Center in Syracuse, New York. Critical of the moral and scientific foundation of psychiatry, Szasz's best-known books include *The Myth of Mental Illness* and *The Manufacture of Madness*. His official web site is www.Szasz.com. This article originally appeared in "The Libertarian Review," in July, 1981.

CHAPTER 7

PRIVATIZING PUBLIC SERVICES

By Robert W. Poole, Jr.

Reminderville, Ohio (pop. 2,000), looks about like any other small, residential town in Middle America. Yet for the past eighteen months, it has received its entire police protection from a private security firm. Not only that, Reminderville's citizens are now paying just half of what they used to pay when the sheriff patrolled the town. And they're receiving a higher level of service.

Yet Reminderville's experience is very much the exception. While privatization is gaining broad acceptance in more conventional public services—garbage collection, street sweeping, park maintenance—somehow the idea of private police officers is difficult for most people to accept. Nevertheless, there are already substantial precedents for obtaining this service, too, by contract.

Consider, first of all, that numerous local governments already purchase their police services from an outside supplier: a neighboring jurisdiction. In Los Angeles County alone, more than two dozen cities contract with the sheriff's department for police services. Altogether, more than sixty California cities obtain their law enforcement services by contract, usually from their sheriff's department. In Connecticut, the state police contract with forty-six towns under a "resident trooper" plan. Similar contracting exists in a dozen other states.

In addition, more and more cities are contracting with private security firms for specialized police services, to free sworn officers for more demanding tasks. St. Petersburg, Florida, has patrolled its parks this way, while Lexington,

Kentucky, has patrolled its public housing projects with private guards.

A nationwide survey by police–management consultants Hallcrest Systems found that 57 percent of all police chiefs and sheriffs would consider contracting out such specialized services as burglar–alarm response. This is a much higher rate of acceptance than existed five or ten years ago. Other services the chiefs would consider farming out include crowd control at special events, bank deposit escorts, prisoner transfer, crime lab work and directing traffic, to name just a few.

Then there's the experience of Switzerland. No wild–eyed radicals, the Swiss seem willing to consider the idea of contract policing. The private firm of Securitas polices more than thirty Swiss villages and townships under contract, offering substantial savings over what it would cost these small towns to operate their own police forces.

Examples of full–fledged police privatization in the United States are rare. While researching nontraditional options in public safety for the Institute for Local Self Government in the 1970s, police researcher Pat Gallagher uncovered the fact that several major security firms— including Guardsmark and Wackenhut—had policed small towns under contract for periods of up to five years. In each case, however, the contract was an interim measure, used by a recently incorporated city just until it could get around to organizing its own police force.

That's the way it turned out for Oro Valley, Arizona. In 1975, the recently incorporated town hired a private firm to replace a contract with the county sheriff's department. Although the company provided quality service at substantial savings, the arrangement was challenged in court by Arizona's law enforcement officers' association, and the company chose not to fight. Today, Oro Valley's conventional police department costs almost four times as much, in real terms, as the contracted private service.

That brings us to Reminderville and its April 1981 contract with Corporate Security, Inc. For $90,000 a year, the town gets the services of seven officers, two patrol cars, and a six–minute response time. The county had demanded $180,000 to provide a single patrol car with a forty–five minute response time. Corporate Security achieves low cost by: (1) paying somewhat lower salaries and fringe benefits than the county sheriff's department, (2) using a less costly (non–civil service) retirement plan, (3) purchasing used but serviceable equipment, and (4) keeping overhead low. The company's employees are all experienced law enforcement personnel; president Arthur Robataille was chief of police of Aurora, Ohio, for fourteen years.

What makes Corporate Security Inc. different from a municipal police agency is the incentives it faces as a profit–seeking entity. Because its revenues depend on remaining cost–effective, the company chose a used Kustom HR–12 radar unit for $350, instead of a new $2,600 model. It also sticks with one–officer patrol cars, which are far more cost––effective than two–officer cars. And its Reminderville chief, Dick Wilk, doubles as the company's electronics technician.

It's precisely this sort of cost–effectiveness that gets ignored when most researchers analyze police privatization. In its 1977 study, "Civilians in Public Safety Services," the Institute for Local Self Government dismissed full police privatization as infeasible because, "There are no secret methods, known only to the private sector, of running an entire police department."

What that statement blithely ignores is the role of incentives in affecting the choices decision–makers end up making. As both the Oro Valley and Reminderville cases make dear, the difference between bureaucratic incentives and profit incentives can be very large, indeed.

Nevertheless, police services are likely to be the last frontier for privatization. Despite the very real prospect of important cost savings, it will take time to overcome people's resistance to the idea. We will not soon see a Buffalo or a Sacramento farming out its entire police operation to a private security firm. (There will probably be more Remindervilles, however—outsourcing by very small towns for whom maintaining their own departments makes no economic sense.)

What we will see is a gradual process of desensitization as people become accustomed to the idea of contracting out services such as parking control and park patrols. "It will be a gradual building process in which the private sector will establish a good track record and prove it can do the job," predicts George Zoley of Wackenhut. "Agencies like ours have to prove ourselves to these departments. But I see a future for it. I think, considering the shortage of government funds, it will be a necessity."

A graduate of M.I.T., Robert Poole founded the Reason Foundation, a nonprofit think–tank advancing free minds and free markets. Poole is now the Director of Transportation Studies at Reason.   Credited with popularizing the term "privatization" for contracting out public service to the private sector, Poole has advised four presidents'administrations on privatization and transportation policy. He is the author of *Cutting Back City Hall* (1980), *Defending a Free Society* (1984), and *Unnatural Monopolies* (1985). This article originally appeared in the *Orange County Register*. Web site: www.Reason.org.

CHAPTER 8

U.S. FOREIGN POLICY VS. THE THIRD WORLD

By Brian Clelland

Even if, like many citizens of the United States, one is dissatisfied with his country's foreign policy, one may believe that the United States is guilty only of bungling, of misguided righteousness, or of a too-ardent concern to police the world in the interest of "security" and "anti-communism." One probably has little idea that recent foreign adventures have been influenced by the imperatives of a rapidly expanding American Empire.[1]

In the process of developing a philosophy which is fully applicable to the entire contemporary world, libertarians must deal much more extensively with a topic that only the left has had the courage to confront—that of the aggressive nature of U.S. foreign policy. Libertarians must make themselves keenly aware that coercive actions undertaken by the U.S. government are not relationships, but rather they encompass virtually the entire globe. Terms such as Pax Americana, the "American Empire" and "United States Imperialism," do, indeed, describe with a high degree of accuracy United States foreign policy throughout the world. For as Murray Rothbard has stated, "(the United States), empirically the most warlike, most interventionist, most imperial government throughout the century."[2]

Undoubtedly, this violently conflicts with the popular image of America as the crusader of freedom, humanitarianism, and goodwill. Such an image is carefully foisted upon the public by the American ruling elites in order to justify the continual aggressive and exploitative expansion of the United States. The popular belief in this façade is evident particularly when Third World nations denounce various United States actions. Almost immediately, public opinion registers very hostile reactions to these statements and, in turn, calls for some form of punitive action be taken to teach those third–rate, pip–squeak nations a lesson. Never is it suggested that perhaps these nations have valid reasons for such hostility, and that they react in this fashion out of a position of frustration and anger at U.S. actions.

These violent feelings toward the U.S. come as a result of the awareness by these nations that they are becoming the recipients of an increasing commitment on behalf of the U.S. to carry out extensive political–economic intervention and penetration. It appears clearly that, in an increasing fashion, the attention of the U.S. (and other industrialized nations, as well) is being focused upon the vast resources of the underdeveloped world. The primary reason for this comes as a result of the rise of new technologies and industrial formations which have produced increasing demand for a multitude of raw resources. Also, there exists within the United States the growing awareness of the limits of our own self–exploitation, insofar as domestic reserves of materials are quickly being exhausted. Consequently, the U.S. has reached outward in search of raw materials, in order to further perpetuate the domestic State–Capitalist system. "Industry now went out into the world in search of the basic material without which in its new forms, it could not exist."[3]

EXPLOITATION OF THE THIRD WORLD

The vast majority of the relationships which have developed between the United States and Third World nations seems predicated upon the process of economic penetration and domination by the United States. For those who hold in high regard individual liberty and economic freedom, it is a sad fact that little attention has been afforded by the United States to the process of development and modernization in these nations—a process which would give rise to viable, self–sustaining economies capable of autonomous action on behalf of the interests of their indigenous populations.

By no means is this meant to suggest that there is an unavoidable link between foreign investment and underdevelopment. Rather, such a relationship exists because U.S. politicians and corporations find it in their interest to establish a dependency existence for the Third World nations. In other words, economic freedom and locally–benefiting development are neither motivational factors nor results of U.S. investment, and if their introduction into the relationship was carried out, the plans and benefits to the U.S. government and corporations would be largely damaged in the process. "Research demonstrates that contemporary underdevelopment is, in large part, the historical product of past and continuing economic and other relations between the satellite underdeveloped and the now–developed metropolitan countries."[4]

To be more specific, just what kind of penetration takes place and how are these relationships perpetuated? First, to a large degree the U.S. has become dependent on foreign sources of raw materials which can easily be labeled "strategic" in nature (e.g., petroleum, bauxite, zinc, lead, and many more). These materials are absolutely vital, insofar as entire industries are predicated on obtaining them at very large costs (which is to be fully expected) and, perhaps more important, that supply should be secured through both political and economic domination, rather than through the use of market actions. While this has produced in the U.S. an illusory situation of abundance, and to some degree is responsible for our disproportionately high level of prosperity, it has also imposed drastic economic distortions upon Third World Nations. Once U.S. investment enters a nation, there is revealed an introduction of various production methods and technologies which, while presenting some advancements to a small portion of an economy, must, by the nature of their limited scope, fail to sustain an economy, once its specific sources or application are no longer profitable enterprises.

An example would be the extraction of a raw material with the use of high, capital–intensive technology. "It would seem indeed, that if such (underdeveloped) countries are to effect a rapid rise in the standard of living, only a small portion of such capital as becomes available should be devoted to the creation of elaborate industrialized equipment, and perhaps none of it to the kind of highly automatized capital–intensive plants...."[5] Moreover, any employment gains will be modest and income derived from such employment will be small, because local labor is usually low–level work; while encouragement of artificially high rates of consumption results in further depletion of the reserves of those nations. Since these nations are usually producers of a very few primary resources, once supplies dwindle or demand drops, their economies are thrown into havoc. Thus, it remains in too many cases that foreign investment is used to direct disadvantage of the underdeveloped nations in the name of economic growth and prosperity for the United States.

CORPORATE PROTECTION BY THE STATE

So far, what has basically been observed is the practice of U.S. corporations, although it is essential that the U.S. government's role in this exploitation be recognized. Insofar as corporations carry out the actual penetration, the fact remains that the political and military clout of the U.S. stands behind the corporations, poised for action should their operation be threatened at any time (remember Chile and the CIA?). While such violent action is exercised rather infrequently, it nonetheless remains part of this government's repertoire of aggression. What appears to be more persuasive a tool in allowing economic penetration is that of foreign aid, in its various forms.

Foreign aid is a much misunderstood policy, insofar as it is commonly viewed as a "giveaway" or "bottomless pit," while, in fact, it is a necessary instrument in America's foreign policy.[6] United States aid programs, by allowing nations to become dependent on the U.S. for various items (e.g., food, military hardware, industrial technology, etc.) place a nation in a precarious position. Accompanying this dependency is increased use of leverage by the United States. Such leverage can be used to maintain "friendly" regimes, to establish and maintain military bases, to assure favorable conditions exist for U.S. corporations to enter these economies, and many other uses.

Once the rhetoric of American politics is stripped away, and a more accurate view of U.S. policy is established vis-à-vis the Third World, it stands as no surprise the open anger, and sometimes rage, which such nations hold for the United States. The type of relationship briefly outlined above treats an interaction which exists and has been historically fostered in the attempt to maintain the economic hegemony of the United States. This is a repressive and reactionary position designed to inhibit adversely the advancement of Third World nations which pose as potential economic and political rivals.

Basically, this means that libertarians should make a firm commitment to a staunch isolationist (non-interventionist) foreign policy based upon national self-determination—whether it be to the left or to the right. Chile, Vietnam, Mayaguez, and other actions have long since removed the U.S. from the role of freedom crusader, and, in turn, have established America as the prime exporter of statist aggression and economic exploitation. The alliance between the U.S. government and corporations has no semblance to free–market actions, and does not deserve the slightest allegiance of any American who believes in political and economic liberty; for, indeed, that is exactly the antithesis of that for which U.S. foreign policy now stands.

Brian Clelland wrote this essay as a position paper published in 1976 by Society for Libertarian Life (SLL), of which he was a member. At the time, Clelland was a student studying foreign affairs at California State University, Fullerton.

---

[1] Magdoff, Harry. *The Age of Imperialism.* (Monthly Review Press, New York: 1969)

2 Rothbard, Prof. Murray N. *For a New Liberty* (MacMillan Company, New York: 1973) p. 287.

3 Magdoff, ibid, p. 32.

4 Frank, Andres Gunder. *Latin America: Underdevelopment or Revolution.* (Monthly Review Press, New York: 1969) p. 4.

5 Von Hayek, Friedrich A. *The Constitution of* Liberty (Henry Regnery Co., Chicago: 1972) p. 367.

6 "Foreign aid—a device for the American taxpayer to subsidize American export industries and foreign governments..." Rothbard, ibid, p. 289.

CHAPTER 9

TAXATION IS THEFT

By David K. Walter

The fundamental rights of any man are the right to life, sustained by freedom of choice, and the right to control the property he earns through his efforts or voluntary exchange with other men.

Any man has the right to defend, by force if necessary, his life, liberty, and property. A man's existence and what he has earned are not the property of others. Man is not a slave to be exploited for the desires, whims, or needs of other individuals. When the property of a man (his life, or that which sustains it) is taken from him by force, the action is known as theft.

One man has taken it upon himself to demand money of persons on the street. If they refuse, he assaults them and takes their money by force. This person is clearly immoral and is a thief. The person robbed is, clearly, a blameless, innocent victim.

In search of bigger game, the man gathers a group of friends who then label themselves the "syndicate." They proceed to terrorize small–businessmen until they turn over "protection" money upon demand. Those who refuse meet with "accidents." Are the actions of this gang any less criminal, simply because there were several persons involved instead of one? The only rational answer is that these actions are not any different—that robbery is robbery and murder is murder—whether committed by one man or by dozens acting in concert.

Finding the syndicate at odds over splitting the loot, our man decides to take a job for a very large gang called the "Internal Revenue Service." He declares that he is an agent of a larger group called the "government," and is empowered to seize money or property to satisfy alleged debts due the "government." Instead of being labeled a thief, our man is now called a "tax collector." He claims it's not for himself that he is taking the money (though he is paid handsomely and bears little risk), but that he is collecting for the "poor" or "defense" or for "the men on the moon." But is he acting any more morally than when he was a lone thief or a member of the gangster syndicate? Like the criminal, the tax collector is taking money or property which does not belong to him, and which the victim does not choose to give voluntarily. If the victim voluntarily supported the cause for which he is being taxed, there would be no need to tax him in the first place. A criminal will seize property if he wishes, and a tax collector will do the same—throwing the victim in jail if he attempts to protect what is his.

It is irrelevant whether a man steals by his own authority or with the sanction of a million others; whether he takes money for himself, or for "the poor," or for any group which did not earn it. Theft consists of taking a man's property against his will, regardless of the beneficiary. If the individual has an inalienable right to his own life, liberty, and property, then morally his life and property are his to do with as he pleases. It is just as immoral for a government to attempt to tax his earnings, regulate his business, or draft his sons, as it would be for some isolated individual acting on his own authority. Associating into a group called government, does not free men from morality, or sanction actions otherwise deemed immoral.

Here arise two myths:

(1) Governments are empowered to do things that individuals are not.

(2) The majority has the right to rule over the minority.

These concepts could lead to dictatorship of the majority and, if carried to their logical extreme, genocide. That which a government may properly do is no different in essence from that which individuals may do. Governments are nothing more than a collection of individuals organized for some purpose—preferably protection. If a single individual does not possess the right to do something, then there is no way that an association of individuals can suddenly acquire this so-called right. All that which is immoral for the individual to do is immoral for a group of individuals to do, no matter how lofty the ends they proclaim, or how divinely inspired they claim their association to be.

Taxes are extorted for projects of which the "taxpayer" does not approve. They cause dislocation of scarce economic resources and retard growth. They enable the state to carry on all manner of anti–freedom activities. They permit the state to manipulate persons, or special interest groups, by helping them or harming them through tax regulations. It has been stated truly, that "the power to tax is the power to enslave."

What is needed is not "tax reform," which is a euphemism for "tax him more and me less"; not more taxes on business, which ultimately, after all, are passed on to the consumer; not more taxes on more products, or on "bad" things like cigarettes, poor housing, or luxury cars; not tariffs or savings bonds or deficit spending or inflation or any other gimmick that politicians devise to hide the magnitude of their theft from the wage earner. What is needed is an end to taxes entirely!

It is argued that taxes are necessary to support services of government. It is claimed that garbage would accumulate knee deep in the streets if trash removal weren't provided by government; that muggers and rapists would roam at will without government police on hand; that the commuter train and bus lines would cease to exist if turned back to private enterprise. Why, we might ask, would men be so foolish as to allow such services to cease without the government's intervention? Do men go barefoot because the shoe industry is still a private operation? Do men forget to report to their jobs every morning because the government does not yet provide them with alarm clocks? Of course not! It is ridiculous to assert that rational men would fail to support voluntarily those services they need if they were not forced to do so. And it is ridiculous, as well as immoral, to force men to support services they do not use and do not value, just because one man, or group of men, think they know what is best for everybody else.

Government services performed today could be provided just as well by free–market entrepreneurs. People would pay for what they desire. No person would be forced to work for the benefit of another (sometimes known as slavery), and no other person could expect to have that person work for him against his will.

Taxation is theft and should be abolished. Government monopolies must be removed so that entrepreneurs can compete freely and make taxation unnecessary. Only then will man truly be able to enjoy the fruits of his labor.

One of the Society for Individual Liberty's (SIL) main founders back in 1969, David Walter is a member of the board of directors of the International Society for Individual Liberty (ISIL). This essay is an excerpt from one of ISIL's early position papers, which was also published in *Society Without Coercion*, edited by Jarret Wollstein. The web site for ISIL is: www.ISIL.org.

CHAPTER 10

CHRISTIAN LIBERTARIANISM

By Rod Boyer

The Israelites had lived and prospered for centuries without a State, but when they asked Samuel for a king, he really laid it on the line: "'your king will take your lands, your children, your goods and your freedom, and you shall cry out in that day."'

A New Dawn for America: The Libertarian Challenge -- Roger L. MacBride, 1976

Christian libertarians are people who believe that the essential tenets of historical Christianity, as presented in the Bible, are, in fact, true. They also believe that libertarianism is the social philosophy morally demanded by the Christian ethic.

THE CHRISTIAN ETHIC

The Christian ethic extends throughout the whole field of human behavior. It is vast, in that it encompasses the complex, interlocking network of all the moral principles which the Bible details. At the same time, it is incredibly simple at its core, and progresses from there in an orderly and reasonable fashion. *"Love the Lord your God with all your heart and with all your soul and with all your mind.* This is the first and greatest Commandment. And the second is like it: *Love your neighbor as yourself.* All the Law

and the Prophets hang on these two commandments." –
Jesus Christ, as recorded in Matthew 22:37.

COERCION VS. LOVE

Christian libertarians believe that coercion is not
consistent with love. For our purposes, coercion can be
defined as "the initiation of force or fraud by one individual
or group against another."

If I love myself (which I do, as all Christians must, if they
are to be enabled to obey the "second greatest
commandment"), then I most certainly don't want to be
victimized by anyone's initiation of force or fraud. According
to the commandment, I must love my neighbor as myself.
This implies that I must also love myself. Love, in the
Christian context, is a decision one makes, a decision to
value someone to an extreme degree. I cannot value myself,
and at the same time, consider the freedom of choice by
which I live and grow to be of little importance.

Christians are commanded to love their neighbors as
themselves.

They believe that God considers all people to be of
extreme importance. They believe God loves people in a very
real and personal sense, and wants them to preserve and
expand their freedom of choice. The Bible is abundant with
exhortations to freedom and warnings against coercion.

THE WORD OF GOD

According to the Old Testament, God's will in terms of
his people is that He alone—*not a government*—should rule
them. This is made explicit in many passages.

It is told that Gideon, a man inspired and empowered by
God, had just saved the Israelites from conquest and
enslavement at the hands of the Midians. The Israelites, in
euphoric gratitude, said, *"Rule over us—you, your son and
your grandson—because you have saved us out of the hand
of Midian."* But Gideon told them, *"I will not rule over you,
nor will my sons rule over you. The Lord will rule over you."* –
Judges 8:22, 23.

For quite some time, the Israelites survived and prospered under God's rule. Just in case some might want to

believe that Israel was ruled by some theocratic government in God's name, Judges 21:25 succinctly reports the fact that there was *no government:* "In those days Israel had no king; everyone did as he saw fit."

Not only did God prefer that we live without a government, He actually saw government as a curse. He eventually allowed the Israelites to form a government, not because they needed one, but to demonstrate to them the devastating consequences of rejecting His solitary rule.

> But when they said, *Give us a king to lead us,* this displeased Samuel; so he prayed to the Lord. And the Lord told him: *Listen to all that the people are saying to you; it is not you they have rejected as their king, but me. As they have done from the day I brought them up out of Egypt until this day, forsaking me and serving other gods, so they are doing to you. Now listen to them; but warn them solemnly and let them know what the king who will reign over them will do.*
>
> Samuel told all the words of the Lord to the people who were asking him for a king. He said, *This is what the king who will reign over you will do: He will take your sons and make them serve with his chariots and horses, and they will run in front of his chariot. Some he will assign to be commanders of thousands and commanders of fifties, and others to plow his ground and reap his harvest, and still others to make weapons of war and equipment for his chariots. He will take your daughters to be perfumers and cooks and bakers. He will take the best of your fields and vineyards and olive groves, and give them to his attendants. He will take a tenth of your grain and of your vintage and give it to his officials and attendants. Your menservants and maidservants and the best of your cattle and donkeys he will take for his own use. He will take a tenth of your flock, and you yourselves will become his slaves. When that day comes, you will cry out for relief from the king you have chosen, and the Lord will*

not answer you in that day.
But the people refused to listen to Samuel.
No! they said, *We want a king over us. Then we will be like all the other nations, with a king to lead us and go out before us and fight our battles.* –1 Samuel 8:6—20.

The idea of God's rule alone is reaffirmed in the New Testament: "We must obey God rather than men!" –Acts 5:29.

As for the question of how there can be peace and order in a society without government, Jesus, in Luke 6:31, gives us the key: "Do unto others as you would have them do to you." This passage has come to be known as the *Golden Rule.* Indeed, it is the gold–standard of Christian ethics. A libertarian society is the only one which can possibly permit the reinstitution of that standard. Ethical bankruptcy is the alternative.

THE PRINCIPLE OF THE THING

Christians are called to live their own lives in an ultimately responsible fashion, resisting the temptations of this world, and turning instead to the glory of God. However, one does not resist temptation by making it illegal, or in some other way coercing its source out of existence. The Christian choice is to turn to God, and to convince others, peacefully, to do likewise. When the choice is removed, one is not resisting temptation, but rather avoiding responsibility.

For these and many reasons, Christian libertarians hold, with all other libertarians, that each individual has the *absolute* right to exercise complete freedom of action, in terms of his own life, liberty, and property, insofar as he permits all others to exercise that same kind of freedom. Christian libertarians are working to expand the recognition of this principle as a social absolute, incapable of being violated with impunity by any individual, group, or government.

Accordingly, we oppose all coercive interference in the marketplace. We call for an end to all forms of involuntary taxation, which we recognize as *legalized theft*. We stand solidly behind the abolition of all laws against victimless crimes, such as drug use, pornography, and prostitution. As Christians, we will continue to oppose strongly such behavior through peaceful persuasion, but we will not forget that salvation is by grace through faith alone; not by jails, guns, and human laws. Accordingly, we call for the immediate release of all persons now incarcerated only for such "crimes." We regard them as political prisoners.

They are behind bars, not because they present a coercive threat to anyone else; they are locked up in cages because they don't conform to the political establishment's idea of proper behavior. Obviously, as Christians, we too must view their behavior as less than holy. However, in the Christian perspective, the behavior of those who put them in jail is completely unjustified.

Jesus set the perfect example for all Christians who want to know how to deal no-coercively with those who sin. The story is recorded in John 8:3–11:

> The teachers of the law and the Pharisees brought in a woman caught in adultery. They made her stand before the group and said to Jesus, *Teacher, this woman was caught in the act of adultery. In the Law, Moses commanded us to stone such women. Now what do you say?* They were using this question as a trap, in order to have a basis for accusing him.
>
> But Jesus bent down and started to write on the ground with his finger. When they kept on questioning him, he straightened up and said to them, *If anyone of you is without sin, let him be the first to throw a stone at her.* Again he stooped down and wrote on the ground.
>
> At this, those who heard began to go away one at a time, the older ones first, until only Jesus was left, with the woman standing there. Jesus straightened up and asked her, *Woman, where are they? Has no one condemned you?*
>
> *No one, sir,* she said.
>
> *Then neither do I condemn you,* Jesus declared. *Go now and leave your life of sin.*

The political establishment said, "Stone her!" Jesus said to her, "neither do I condemn you. Go now and leave your life of sin." Peaceful, loving persuasion—not coercion—is the Christian libertarian method.

We believe that our work as Christian libertarians is in obedience to both God and reason. There is, indeed, hope for liberty in our time.

One of the original leaders of Society for Libertarian Life (SIL) at California State University at Fullerton, Rod Boyer wrote this article in the 1970's as a student working toward a degree in psychology and divinity. In later years Boyer became involved with the Libertarian Party, and ran in 2002 for U.S. Congress in the 45th District (Palm Springs, California).

CHAPTER 11

JUSTICE: A LIBERTARIAN OUTLOOK

By L.K. Samuels

...before laws were made, there were relations of possible justice. To say that there is nothing just or unjust but what is commanded or forbidden by positive laws, is the same as saying that before the describing of a circle all radii were not equal.

Charles de Montesquieu (1689–1755)

The definition of justice and how to apply it are perhaps the most crucial and elusive questions facing mankind. Libertarians and voluntarists vary on meanings, alternatives, and applications to remedy injustice, compensate victim(s), judge criminals, and punish the guilty. Only a few of the many libertarian approaches to justice will be discussed here.

WHAT IS JUSTICE?

For centuries, the Western concept of justice has been based on the principle of *suum cuique* (meaning "to each his own"). Western legal codes vary little on the concept of rendering to each person what is rightfully his or hers. It is the question of *what* belongs to *whom* which often must be decided through some form of arbitration.

To the libertarian, *suum cuique* is the basis of justice. However, as many know, the Western legal code has caused a great injustice, by breaking its own rule when government becomes involved. The legal code says, in effect, that if someone steals another person's property, it shall be returned and the thief punished—unless, of course, the thief is the government. In that case, the victim(s) of the crime shall be fined and imprisoned if they have resisted government seizure of their rightful property. The Western legal code system thus has created a double standard for justice. Under the current system, theft is theft, unless it is government committing the crime.

Although it was in the private sector, in mercantile communities of Europe centuries ago, that justice and law developed, government has taken control of the definition and execution of justice. In other words, the legal code system is operated by government, to benefit and protect government. It is the State which possesses almost sole authority over definition, process, and execution of justice. Is that just and equitable?

AN APPROACH TO JUSTICE

Many libertarians argue that justice should be privatized, that is, treated like any other commodity or service in the marketplace. Individual consumers, juries, and judges not employed by the government should determine what is just and unjust. No form of justice should ever be allowed to be operated and manipulated politically, as is being done today. Currently, judges must follow legislated laws passed by politicians. It is not beyond the realm of possibility to suggest that political leaders constantly pass legislation not for fairness and equity, but for political consideration.

For these reasons, judges should neither be appointed by politicians nor elected through the political system, but selected through the open marketplace by consumers.

The legal code system should not be legislated, but should be discovered through the interaction of jurors, judges, and trials. As today, the legal system would generally follow prior court decisions to assist in determining a just verdict. The consumer (along with his or her insurance company) would determine priority of the crimes to be prosecuted. That is, a client, by paying for personal protection and insurance, would determine from which crime he or she most wants protection. For example, a client could purchase more rape protection and less robbery protection, depending on individual choice. It would be the consumer, through privatized protection systems, who would determine protection needs.

As for *victimless crimes,* at present it is the consumer who must pay directly for programs to locate, arrest, try, and jail individuals accused of dealing in drugs, prostitution, gambling, and so forth. Libertarians oppose laws against victimless "crimes," but under a totally free–market justice system, consumers—not the State—would determine what constitutes law and justice. It is unlikely that even a zealous moralist would be willing to pay thousands of dollars in lawyer, court, and insurance fees to prosecute prostitutes or pot smokers. However, when the State is involved in prosecuting victimless–crime laws, it has virtually unlimited tax funds to interfere in people's personal lives. Under free–market justice, the victim (or relatives, or insurance companies) would bring charges, not the state.

JUSTICE AND THE POOR

The poor would benefit most from freeing the legal system from the grip of politics. Generally, it is the poor individual in ghetto sections of town who has no political influence. Therefore, the police provide little protective service. And when the police are present, they are more of a hazard than a help. Minorities are often victimized by the government police, and the poor have no other means of defense than to protect themselves.

Since services in the free market cost about half as much as such government services, the poor could now afford some type of privatized protection. This might range from a security guard being stationed on the block, to installation of electronic burglar alarms. If fees are too high for very impoverished persons, they could buy short–range protection plans, or just thumb through the yellow pages to call help when they need it. Still others could take advantage of low–cost or even *free* legal clinics established by charitable groups.

The point: the poor get little protection from the government police, and when the police *are* present, all too often they are busting pot–smokers, jaywalkers, bookies, and strippers, while overlooking or even ignoring their responsibility to prevent violent crimes. This is because the government pays the police directly from taxpayers' funds. Libertarians would like to see the police being paid directly by consumers, with the option to buy from many policing services or not to buy any protection at all.

PACIFIST JUSTICE

Some libertarians, such as Robert LeFevre, endorse a pacifist approach to justice. First, LeFevreians argue that there is no such thing as justice, only *honored contracts* and *broken contracts*. Second, they argue that preventive measures to ensure protection of life and property are superior to vengeful search, arrest, and prosecution of criminals.

A similar approach is employed by corporations in white–collar crimes. A corporation, for instance, usually does not attempt to capture and prosecute an embezzling employee. To attempt capture and arrest is considered wasting good money in an almost hopeless attempt to retrieve *bad money* (stolen money). This is not a moral judgment; often it is simply economically more practical to forget past losses and concentrate on preventive measures.

A strong majority of libertarians, however, favor strong prosecution of criminals to deter future crimes. Most libertarians agree that justice can be achieved by capturing the criminal and making him or her compensate the victim(s)—or relatives—of a violent crime or fraud. In this, libertarian theory differs, from traditional theories and practices to dealing with criminals, prisons, and compensation to the victim.

RESTITUTION

Currently, Western legal codes ignore the restitution side in criminal cases. During criminal procedures, the legal battle is between the State (People vs. ...) and the criminal, not between the victim and the accused. The victim is ignored. If the victim wants to collect damages from the criminal, he or she must first wait for a guilty verdict, and then (at the victim's own expense) file a civil suit to recover damages.

However, changes are in the wind. In Minnesota, for instance, Judge Dennis Challen of the Winona County Court, has developed a "self–sentencing program emphasizing restitution. The record is remarkable. Since 1972, more than 3,000 misdemeanants have gone through Challen's restitution program. Burglars work for those they burglarized, auto thieves locate the owner of the auto they stole; and vandals repair the damage they caused. And the repeat rate is only two percent as compared with 50–70 nationally."

Some studies on restitution have researched the idea of a "time/work sentence." That is, when a criminal is convicted, a monetary restitution sum could be set. When those funds have been paid back to the victim in full, the criminal is released. The criminal has the option to work more hours (overtime) to pay restitution fees. This approach encourages the criminal to learn a skill and develop good working habits. It also helps to alleviate the overcrowding in jails.

PRIVATIZED PRISONS

One approach being considered is the idea of contracting prison operations to private firms. In 1974, Minnesota's state laws were changed to permit private industry to operate prisons. The results were encouraging.

In Minnesota's privatized Lino Lakes Prison, prisoners are able to work for substantial wages. Prisoners such as Sam Johnson work as apprentice upholsterers, making $2.50 per hour (1977) for Furniture Workshop, Inc. This may seem a small salary, but most government–operated prisons pay inmates less than a dollar per day, while most inmates work an average of three and a half hours per day. Furthermore, Johnson pays $120 a month to the state for his room and board. Lino Lakes Prison also provides jobs in the manufacturing of rope, farm equipment, and snowmobiles, and in metal finishing.

Even Richard L. Mitchell, former chief program administrator of the New York Department of Correctional Services, has proposed a contractual private prison plan. He wrote, "Prisons as now structured simply do not attract the kind of innovative professionals who can create new ways of doing things. For better or worse, talent gravitates in our society towards profit."

TO INSURE JUSTICE

Preventive measures are usually the best approach to any problem. Libertarians have suggested that one possible way to insure justice would be to purchase an insurance policy covering loss of life and property. Of course, such coverage is already available and on the market in the form of life, auto, homeowner's, and renter's insurance, but such insurance could be taken a step further. A "bounty/restitution" insurance policy could assist in deterring crime, and thus could help create a more just society.

The bounty/restitution policy could insure against injury to life and property, and then automatically set up a bounty of, say, $200,000 or so for the person who provides information which leads to the arrest and conviction of a thief or murderer. The insurance company then could offer a million–dollar bounty on all convicted murderers of the policyholder; and since insurance companies would rather not pay high claims, they could offer cash rewards of between $5,000 and $50,000 to anyone who is responsible for preventing or halting violent crimes like muggings, rapes, thefts, and assaults. If bounty/restitution insurance were to become popular, it could transform everyone into "instant bodyguards." The normally shy passer–by would jump into action if he witnessed a crime in progress, hoping to cash in on a hefty reward. Presently, there is no incentive to deter a crime in progress. Considering the danger of injury, and the likelihood that the caught criminal might be set free on some courtroom technicality, there is no reason to prevent a crime in progress. But with cash rewards, crime could be reduced drastically.

There is a possible abuse associated with a bounty

system: mob reprisal against an accused criminal. To prevent this abuse, a stipulation could be added to the policy to warn that any person or persons found to have harmed or killed an alleged criminal will automatically have a bounty placed on them. Such a stipulation would motivate bounty hunters to bring back an alleged criminal in good health; otherwise, if the alleged criminal is found "not guilty," the company offering the award could be sued for having harmed an innocent person.

CAPITAL PUNISHMENT

Libertarians vary on the issue of capital punishment. A privatized justice system might actually allow for capital punishment in extreme cases. However, under a restitution system, it is unlikely, although possible, that victim(s), jury, and judge would issue a death penalty verdict. The reason is clear. A death verdict cannot bring back loved ones; but the murderer's labor for the rest of his or her life can give partial restitution to the victim's dependents. Executing a convicted murderer provides only the satisfaction of revenge. Why should it be society who bears the financial burden of orphans, widows, and widowers? The criminal, and no one else, should pay the cost of his crime.

THE CLASH: STATE VS. NON–STATE JUSTICE

One major problem with a non–government legal system is that government would most likely prohibit it. Government gains an enormous advantage when justice and the legal system are operated by the State. It is doubtful that any government would willingly surrender that monopoly.

Some libertarians have suggested that, under certain circumstances, a privatized justice system could remedy this problem. They say that a private justice system could compete effectively with the government's system. Since the government's system takes longer and costs more, more consumers would participate in the privatized system. However, with two systems, unfortunately, citizens would be paying twice for justice, since governmental services are funded via mandatory taxation.

Other libertarians suggest that to halt this double

payment, a more direct course must be taken. Since taxation is immoral in the first place, they argue, it is moral to defend one's property from individual and governmental thieves. These libertarians suggest that a campaign to scare off tax collectors would be the best approach to make it difficult for the government to collect taxes or to hire more tax collectors. Prior to the American Revolution, colonists would often run King George's tax collectors out of town on a rail (frequently tarred and feathered, too). The practice was so widespread that the king could not hire enough tax collectors. Eventually, few colonists paid any taxes at all. It has been estimated that those colonists who did pay taxes, paid no more than one or two percent of their personal income; a far cry from the 40 to 50% being taken by the United States government today.

Some have suggested tax–avoidance over tax–evasion, while others suggest forming churches and taking a "vow of poverty." Still others urge political legislation and initiatives to bring about a free system of justice and law.

CONCLUSION

Whatever the method, the day will come when justice will not be manipulated politically.   The legal system should be treated like any other commodity or service. If justice is to work, it must be free of politics and red tape. The consumer must gain greater control over justice and the legal system.

The manager and co–manager of the Future of Freedom Conference series for five years in the 1980's, L.K. Samuels is a writer and libertarian activist. He founded Society for Libertarian Life (SLL) at the California State University, Fullerton in the early 1970's. He was instrumental in forming Rampart Institute, based on the works of Robert LeFevre.   Former Northern Vice Chair of the Libertarian Party of California (2003-2007), he has authored a series of fiction and nonfiction books. Web site: www.Freedom1776.com. This article was published in the 1970s as a position paper for SLL

CHAPTER 12

THE CASE FOR PRIVATIZING PROTECTIVE SERVICES

By James Gallagher

Very few crimes are committed in the presence of police.

–Robert LeFevre, 1978

Human beings in organized societies have naturally specialized in the function of self–defense. So that individuals may go about their affairs without having to commit great effort and resources to protection of their life, limb, and property from predators (both human and non–human), we arrange for trusted agencies to act in our behalf when we become subject to aggression. Unfortunately, all too often the agencies charged with the defense duties have themselves turned out to be the tyrants of history. So it is (and always has been) with police agencies of the state.

PUBLIC PROTECTION SERVICE: THE PROBLEM

Very few of us are satisfied with the services received from our various police departments. Coupled with apparent impotence when faced with criminals, police systematically harass innocent citizens for driving faster than some arbitrary speed, using substances classified as "illegal," selling these substances, selling and buying sexual or sex–related services, gambling, or providing a vast array of products and services without government permission. Further, we are presented with enormous expenditures and taxes for these same harassments.

The citizen feels impotent, because there seems to be no alternative available. Why must this be? Police departments are rewarded where they achieve their greatest successes. The easiest "successes" available to police are those areas where they encounter the least resistance and skill. The "speeder" is easy prey to an armed officer with $40,000 worth of equipment. The difficulty in arresting the prostitute or the pot–smoking worker is minimal, and police departments allocate large amounts of resources and personnel to the area where they can show "results. "

The adult service–providing bookstore proprietor is easily hounded from pillar to post, because he must operate visibly. Meanwhile, the true crime rate, that is, crimes against property and violence, soars, and the poor suffer the most. This has come to be regarded as "highway justice."

The most persuasive influence on our society by the police comes at the hands of these modern–day "highwaymen." It is changing the way the people regard their "protectors." The barrage of television propaganda ("CHIPS," "The Rookies," etc.) is a conscious attempt to neutralize the natural resentments people feel. In public schools, children are taught to accept these injustices as "necessary" to public order. Students of history will recognize these tactics from accounts of life in Nazi Germany in the 1930's.

PRIVATE PROTECTION SERVICE: A SOLUTION

The missing element in acquiring satisfactory protection services seems to be the absence of the free market. If the user could choose from whom to buy, the seller of these services would be forced to satisfy their customers or perish. Are there not private security agencies on the market? Yes; however, they do not have the advantage of a coercive tax base from which to control the market. They are also prohibited from those activities which do not constitute protection from crimes against persons or their property. Quite correctly, all should be prohibited from such activities.

CASE HISTORY: MANAGUA, NICARAGUA

The *Guardia Nacional* was the state–run agency in the Central American country of Nicaragua. This agency was well–armed and also served as the country's army. The army was loyal to dictator General Anastasio Somoza (who ruled from 1967 to 1979). It was composed mostly of uneducated and poorly paid peasants, and corrupt officers who augmented their small salaries with graft and special privileges. Protection of property and person was given only to the influential few.

In poor and lower-middle-class neighborhoods, the residents formed local committees to provide for their own protective services. Guards were stationed every two blocks in each direction, and the guards' salaries were paid by those residents within one block of the guard station. Each guard carried a flashlight, a whistle, a night stick, and if he could afford it, a handgun.

At prescribed intervals these guards would signal their counterparts two blocks away to show all was well. In the event of an intrusion, the guards would rouse the residents or run the intruder(s) off, whichever seemed prudent. The crime rate was very low in that area. The price/performance ratio was unmatched by anything that could be provided by the government–operated protective services.

CASE HISTORY: PARADISE ISLAND, BAHAMAS

The intrusion of the State on the private lives of its citizens is yet minimal in the Bahamas, although it is getting worse. There are, as yet, no taxes on income, aside from a social security tax amounting to a maximum of $10 per month. Government funding is provided mostly by customs duties.

The police force is primarily a group of attractively dressed men who direct traffic and pose for tourists' photographs. All serious protective services are provided by private companies. At Paradise Island, a complex of hotels and resort facilities including a high–income casino, all police–related activities are provided by Security Services, Ltd.

These private guards are mostly semi–retired men and women of high moral caliber, who earn not only a supplement to their retirement incomes, but supplement their sense of self–worth as well. Their equipment includes inexpensive Rambler Hornets, and weapons are carried only for armored and high–risk services.

The resources of this company are limited to sixty or seventy guards, a few vehicles, three or four administrative people, and a guard captain. These resources are sufficient to serve twenty–five to thirty companies, as well as Paradise Island Ltd. Since they have taken responsibility for the protective service of the island, they have had one of the best records in the world for low incidence of theft, rape, and assault in a tourist area. They enjoy the flexibility of providing varying levels of service according to the value placed by the customer on security in a given area.

By way of contrast, theft and assault are becoming major problems on the Bahamas' main island of New Providence, which also depends heavily on tourism.

A FREE MARKET ALTERNATIVE

What can be done?

It can be seen that the quality of services provided by a protective agency will depend on whether the user has the option to secure another agency in the event that the present supplier is in some way unsatisfactory. Users of public services are required to pay for the service whether or not they use it. A step in the direction of more satisfactory protective services might be to place local government services on a completely self–supporting basis, in competition with privately provided services. This way, the user could contract for whatever level of services he or she required.

Ultimately, it is apparent that government–provided services will lose adherents, because of their innate inability to compete on an equal basis either with companies committed to making a profit, or with other voluntary organizations such as co–ops and neighborhood self-protection associations.

A programmer in the early days of the computer industry, James Gallagher worked for IBM in Nicaragua for over four years in the 1960's. After returning to the United States, he established his own consultancy firm, James Gallagher and Associates, which developed easy–to–learn data-entry systems. Active in the Libertarian Party of Orange County, he ran as a candidate for the California State Assembly. This essay comes from a Society for Libertarian Life position paper first published in 1979.

CHAPTER 13

THE FREE PORTS OF EARTH: FLOATING CITIES OF SEA AND SPACE

By Gary C. Hudson

In many places in libertarian literature, we find reference to the inviolate sanctuary, the hidden community to which freedom–seeking individuals may repair. From *Atlas Shrugged* to *The Probability Broach*, it is a recurrent ideal. Regrettably, it has never been fulfilled in reality.

Equally interesting, yet also flawed, are schemes such as tax–free havens and libertarian revolutions in developing countries. Reality has slapped libertarian thinkers in the face many times in the last few years. Is it time to consider another tack, given that libertarian goals and ideals seem far removed from the realities of American democratic politics?

About a decade ago, I began to investigate the idea of space–oriented free ports. The concept was brought to mind by a quotation from Arthur C. Clarke's *The Promise of Space,* in which he waxes poetic on future manned space stations in synchronous orbit:

> *They will be able to look up at the night sky and watch the stately procession of the Ports of the Earth—the strange new harbours where the ships of space make their planetfalls and departures. Often, one of these brightly orbiting stars will suddenly explode in a silent concussion of light, and a fierce,*

tiny sun will draw slowly away from it. And they will know that some nuclear–powered mariner has set forth once more, on the ocean whose farther shore he can never reach.

Clarke's poetry evoked powerful images in my mind. One of them lingers to this day.

If there are floating worlds in space, who will build them? Who will need them? Who will rule them? It seemed that there needed to be an answer to the last question before there could be an answer to the first. This simple observation, coupled with the escapist desire for a libertarian sanctuary, led me inexorably to the conclusion that the Ports of Earth should be *free* ports. How else could commerce be made to flourish, as liberty is maintained?

Yet we must also learn to walk before we run. The technological hurdles associated with the development of space cities are significant, to say nothing of the financial problems developers must face. This is not to say that such communities will not be built within the lifetimes of most of those who read these words, but rather that we must expect their establishment as outgrowths of similar cities here on earth.

Where would one expect to build such cities on earth? If they are located within the boundaries of existing nation–states, there is every expectation that a libertarian ideal would not be the guiding philosophy behind either their establishment or their governing. For example, many "new towns" have been built in the U.S. during the past twenty years. Irvine, California, Las Colinas outside Dallas, and even Florida's Disney World are all useful models for the physical architects of cities, but not for the philosophical architects.[1]

---

[1] Disney World, however, may be in part a model for a first-stage Libertarian community. The thousands of Disney acres are governed in traditional fashion, but every one of the voters, supervisors, and other "government" employees of the Disney "county" is a Disney employee. A special act of the Florida legislature gives the Disney management virtual sovereignty over their property, including the right to build nuclear power reactors, if they so choose, to generate their electrical power.

If we cannot look to building our city on existing U.S. land, we probably cannot expect the situation to be much better in other countries. It has been argued that there is an incentive for a poor, third–world country to permit the establishment of a free zone to enhance trade and economic benefits to the host country. Rarely, however, has any nation freely given up sovereignty over its soil. Even measurable economic benefits might not produce the desired effect on the part of the host country. Given these political realities, I believe that we must turn to land unknown by anyone: the sea.

This might appear to be a *non sequitur.* Land on the sea? Many nations have reclaimed ocean as land by means of fill: the Dutch are among the masters of such reclamation.

Proposals for large offshore islands for industrial purposes (such as the sitting of nuclear power reactors) have been suggested in this country and abroad. Even airports have been built on fill.

The only major difficulty with a reclaimed island structure is the legal status. If located within the 200–mile economic limit or the 12–mile legal limit, the reclaimed land, or any built structure which rests on the ocean floor, would immediately come under the jurisdiction of the nation bordering the island. Attempting to build a polder in deep waters beyond the 200–mile limit would be a formidable technological challenge.

As an alternative, I propose a freely floating city–island, located outside the 12–mile limit, but within the 200–mile limit. This city–island would be a libertarian free port whose primary revenue and economic base would come from service industries such as banking, commodities, medical care, education, trade, and retailing, rather than from manufacturing or agricultural businesses.

There must be some incentive for the host country and state (in my scenario, the U.S. and California, assuming the location of the city island to be just off Long Beach) to permit the establishment of the city and support of its continued existence. One set of potential incentives involves the provision to the mainland of services which are in great demand.

Several such services could be foreseen. The state of

California, and especially the city of Los Angeles, will
require a larger amount of fresh water during the late
1980's and 1990's than can be supplied via existing
sources. Fresh water, created from nuclear–driven
desalinators (unlikely to be built in the U.S. due to
pressures by radical environmentalists), could be supplied
to the mainland, along with electrical power off–loaded from
the reactors. Fusion or, ultimately, satellite solar power
could be used in place of nuclear fission, though at the
expense of waiting a decade or two for the necessary
technological advances.

Another potential service incentive is transportation. Los
Angeles International Airport is overcrowded, and is not
going to get any better, even with the new terminal
construction. There is just not enough room for new
runways and service buildings within the confines of the
present airport. If a floating airport were to be built
adjoining the city–island, there is every likelihood that such
a facility could draw long–haul international traffic off the
existing airport, reducing its burden and saving the city,
state, and federal governments the expense of building a
new airport. Likewise, the establishment of docks and
tanker terminals at the city–island would be a way of off–
loading existing crowded ports along the Southern
California coast.

In addition, the city–island would attract gamblers and
fun–seekers from Las Vegas. The state of California would
welcome the chance to "keep money and jobs in the state,"
since many of the workers on the city–island would
probably live in Los Angeles. Tourists to the island would
likely stop off for a few days in Southern California, as well.

Viewed from this perspective, a floating free–port city
becomes not only a challenge technologically, but also a
relatively straightforward real estate project—albeit a
massive one. After being in business for a few years, it
would begin to attract capital and talent to the true
libertarian environment it offers. At that stage, it would
become the center of financial and technical support for the
establishment of other floating cities near other countries
and in space. As the center of a network of libertarian city–
states, it would become the focus for freedom–loving
individuals everywhere. As such, it could become the most

effective check upon the excesses of government ever implemented.

Founder of Rotary Rocket Company and AirLaunch LLC, Gary Hudson has been active in developing innovative aerospace propulsion systems. He is the designer of the Phoenix VTOL/SSTO family of launch vehicles, and has worked with General Dynamics and Boeing Aerospace on single–stage–to–orbit launch vehicles. A Fellow of the British Interplanetary Society, Hudson received the "Laurel Award" from *Aviation Week & Space Technology* "for the vision, drive and competence that has pushed to the front of the U.S. launcher agenda." He has taught launch vehicle design to graduate students at Stanford University. In the 1980's he spoke at the Freeland Conference about the possibility of using space technology to establish libertarian colonies away from a government–controlled earth, and this article developed from that talk. His web site is www.AirLaunchLLC.com.

CHAPTER 14

WHAT ABOUT THE POOR?

By L.K. Samuels

I do not know of a single example of a predominantly collectivist or centrally planned society in which the ordinary citizen has achieved a major and substantial improvement in the condition of his everyday life or a real hope for the future of himself or his children.

Professor Milton Friedman, Nobel Prize
Laureate in economics, 1976

It is said that people, especially the poor, cannot provide for their own well–being, and therefore, that anti–poverty programs operated by government agencies must be created. But does government really help the poor, or does government create economic and psychological poverty?

A few examples are in order.

A special government program, operated by the Small Business Administration, "handed out millions of dollars to help 3,400 minority small businesses over the past ten years—and only about thirty are still in business today." (*National Enquirer*, Feb. 27, 1979). Despite generous loans and loose contracts, government's effort to increase wealth and jobs failed.

Another example: a woman in Watts, California, received an eviction notice. Mrs. Moore, a 53–year–old hospital clerk, was told by the State of California her home had been sold for $173. Under the Improvement Act of 1911, which was intended to give California cities an easy way to improve neighborhood streets, property owners have thirty days to pay an assessment. If they do not, the city treasurer's office sells the unpaid bill to anyone interested. In 1971, the city installed streetlights on Mrs. Moore's street, and assessed the residents.

When she had asked a local city councilman about the length of time required for payment, he had told her that she had ten years in which to pay. The new owners now wanted $6,000 for the duplex home.

This is not an isolated case. In one year alone, some 143 persons lost their homes to this law in Los Angeles. It is not the rich who are victimized by such laws. (*Associated Press*; June 15, 1977).

Take the plight of Mrs. Flora Thorpe, a 59–year–old widow in Cleveland. After resorting to pawning her wedding ring to pay for a new roof just to comply with city housing codes, she was jailed anyway. City inspectors arrested the otherwise law-abiding widow after she said she could not afford to have her house painted, too. Mrs. Thorpe explained to city officials that if it weren't for the small dog-breeding business she was conducting in her home, she would starve. The city officials cited her for that, too. Mrs. Thorpe needed help; instead, she got government. (*United Press International*; May 1, 1973).

WHAT ABOUT THE POOR?

The first question that inevitably pops into one's mind when first confronted with libertarian alternatives is, *What about the poor?* For some reason, it appears to many people that libertarians feel nothing for the poor; otherwise, why would they oppose welfare, Medicare, and food stamps? Those of a more altruistic persuasion shriek with horror when told that government is not the answer to minimizing poverty. Altruists would rather think of libertarians as heartless brutes who would seize bread from hungry children, or wrest white canes from the blind. "Why," they scream, "without welfare and the taxes to support it, everyone would be impoverished!"

In the first place, government does not produce the bread we eat, or manufacture white walking canes for the blind. Poverty can be reduced only by increasing production of food, housing, and other goods. Government, however, by its very nature, does not produce anything. The only thing the government knows about the marketplace is how to regulate it. If the State tries to produce a product or service, citizens are given a product with all the quality of the U.S. Postal Service and Keystone Cops rolled up in one. Government is a strain on the economy, slowing it down with regulations, resulting in fewer jobs, higher prices, and less productivity.

Poverty is not only economic in nature. When roads to personal achievement and acquisition of wealth are blocked, frustration and feelings of helplessness set in, creating a sense of failure in the individual. Welfare, too, can promote a sense of failure—a poverty of the spirit and an unwillingness to move forward in business ventures and self–improvement. In such an environment, the individual becomes trapped by his subconscious fears and insecurity. After all, he is accepting handouts, which, to many people, proves that he can do nothing but fail.

For this reason, education in self–improvement has become a major tool in undermining poverty. As an old American Indian saying goes: "Give a man a fish and he eats for a day; teach a man to fish and he eats forever."

PHONEY LAWS

But what about governmental laws designed to assist the poor?

They usually accomplish the exact opposite. As Professor Murray Rothbard, in an interview in *Penthouse* (October, 1975), pointed out, "The laws to help the poor are phoney. The poor don't really benefit from the welfare state."

In the article, Rothbard cited a study of a ghetto district in Washington, D.C. "After estimating the taxes those people paid to the federal government and balancing that figure against the money the federal government gives back to them, it turned out that they are getting less from the government than they are giving. They're paying for the welfare state just as much as everybody else! The money is simply siphoned off into the military–industrial complex, into bureaucratic salaries, and so forth."

The 1968 report from the Tax Foundation showed that national, state, and local taxes take 34 percent of the income of individuals who earn less than $3,000 a year. (*U.S. News & World Report*; Dec. 9, 1968). Current studies from the Tax Foundation show that the poor continue to pay a good portion of their salaries into the tax collector's coffer. Perhaps if the impoverished and middle class did not pay so much in taxation, they could afford less expensive services from the private sector, instead of those services now provided by government.

Another law which hurts the poor is the Minimum Wage Law. In April, 1972, a report by the National Federation of Independent Businesses stated that a "loss of 680,000 jobs for marginal and submarginal workers...not to mention job opportunities that did not develop"...followed that year's minimum wage increase.

Everybody wants higher wages, but, as Professor Henry Hazlitt once wrote, "We cannot make a man worth a given amount by making it illegal for anyone to offer him less."

If minimum wage laws, taxes, and regulations do not drain the pocketbook and make workers eligible for the breadline, then inflation surely will. As government inflates the money supply, so does the dollar decrease in value. Worse yet, as the worker's income increases, his purchasing power declines.

This is only half of the story. The progressive Federal Income Tax works the same way. As a worker's income increases, so does his percentage of taxable income. The worker is making more money on paper, but is unable to buy more products at the supermarket; and he is paying at a higher, ever increasing rate of taxation. In 1975, the Department of Labor reported that "an average worker in private industry, supporting a family of four, now pays 23.4 percent more to the federal government for income tax and Social Security than he did a year ago." (*A.P.*; October 4, 1976). In other words, in 1975, taxes increased more than gasoline and food prices combined. This is amazing, considering that many people look upon the oil and food industries as being run by rip–off artists. Probably 50 percent of the price increases in these industries was due primarily to higher taxes being levied on those businesses. It is government which is the real rip–off artist. Not only do workers pay double the price for government and the problems it creates, but they don't even get a loaf of bread or a tank of gasoline.

ALTRUISTIC SCROOGE

If the government were prohibited from engaging in charity, who would care for the poor? This question implies the assumption that only government will provide for those who are poor; which, of course, is untrue. People take care of people, because as social creatures, it is our nature to help others in time of need. Besides the psychological urge to help others, people feel an instinctive compassion towards the needy—and Americans do in a big way. In 1973 alone, private charities in the United States received a total of $24.5 billion in voluntary contributions, an increase of nine percent over the previous year. Moreover, the ordinary individual accounted for three–fourths of the 1973 total. (*U.S. News & World Report*; April 8, 1974) Five years later, in 1978, Americans donated $39.6 billion to charity. (*Newsweek*; May 7, 1979)

Altruists would have us believe that everyone is heartless and unwilling to help those in difficulties. However, if the average citizen were asked to help a needy person, most would, indeed, help. What makes the altruist so certain that nobody would? Perhaps the altruist is an Ebenezer Scrooge in disguise. Perhaps he has a bad conscience or a guilt complex. He does not want to assist the needy himself, and so feels regret. Instead of working with the poor, helping them better themselves with deeds and action, the altruist attends congressional cocktail parties to lobby for legislation that will force someone else to be charitable for him.

Sy Leon, author of *None of the Above,* once observed, "There are three ways to help people: (1) you can help other people yourself; (2) you can persuade people to help other people; (3) you can force people to help other people." The first two are completely within the bounds of a free society; but the third is based on the authority of police, soldiers, and guns.

The point is: people cannot be forced to be charitable. Sure, the tax money is collected at the point of a gun, but the giver is resentful of the receiver. This is not true charity—it is forced charity. It is theft from those who pay, and demeaning to those who have had, for generations, little choice but to accept government handouts.

The socialist solution to poverty, even though it fails, is to redistribute wealth in equal proportions. At first, socialists and equalitarians were satisfied with voluntary means to achieve this equalization of wealth distribution. However, they became impatient when equalization did not just happen automatically. This led them to advocate confiscation of wealth from individuals—using government as the mandatory collecting agency.

The problem with using government to correct the inequalities in wealth is twofold. First, to use the state in such a manner is to play into the hands of ambitious political movements. Any law or punishment imposed to achieve such a noble sounding goal may be justified on the premise that the *means justify the end*. This encourages legislation which would violate human and individual rights as the state centralizes, to make equalization of wealth more practical. The results are: the state centralizes; political leaders get to play Caesar; and special interest groups obtain their dose of power. By this time, the needy are lost in the political shuffle.

Secondly, it is futile to strive for equalization of wealth. Equality of any sort is not only elusive, it is impossible to achieve or maintain for any length of time. It goes against the nature of reality. Nature does not provide any strong example of equality in human beings or in the animal world. Each species in the animal world has unique means for self–protection, concealment, and gathering food. Each species has different, unequal abilities and body functions to survive. Some animals developed hard shells to ward off predators. Others developed wings to escape larger animals on the ground. Still others have great running power to out–run enemies. Equality is strikingly absent in nature. It is far more in accordance with nature to strive for self–improvement, than to enforce an artificial equality.

GOVERNMENT DICTATIONS

The next result is predictable. In a democratic nation, as productivity declines and government programs fall behind schedule, the planners of equality soon realize that they are in danger of losing credibility. As the poverty–stricken people demand action, government planners must resort to primitive, naked force. The state nationalizes industry and workers as though everything the state touches is a national resource. Rebellious workers are then transferred to menial jobs or fired. And with government being the sole employer, a dissatisfied worker could find it difficult to feed his or her family.

Forced equality eventually leads to centralization of authority, underproduction, less food, lack of housing, and unemployment which, in effect, institutionalizes poverty and subservience.

INEQUALITY OF THE COIN FLIPS

Let's set that aside for the moment, and let's suppose someone did create the perfect society, in which every individual shared or received an equal amount of wealth. Also suppose that John and William met and decided to flip a coin in a dollar bet. Once the coin is flipped and the winner, William, takes his prize, equality has vanishes—William has more wealth than John. To prevent this, the planners of equality would have to prohibit John and William—and everyone else—from engaging in betting or trading activity. Wealth is bred from trade. Without trade, everyone would starve, naked and cold. Even in the most socialistic nations, trade is the basic fabric of society. Equalitarian theories are just that—theories.

There's more: enforced equality assumes that *value* is *objective,* that an object or action has one value. But value is so very *subjective,* not objective at all.

A good wage to one person is a low wage to another. A high price to one customer is a low price to another. People place different values on everything. Equality of wealth cannot be achieved, because beyond a small number of people, nobody can agree on what is equal. Usually, some equality is achieved when two people agree to make a trade. When the trade is made, each trader sees an opportunity to trade a lesser subjective value for a higher one. A shopper would buy a bag of potatoes for a dollar only because, to him, ten potatoes represent a higher value compared to the dollar, a lower value. Otherwise, it is doubtful that an exchange would have been made. Clearly, these values are set by the two traders—not by government planners.

No wonder chaos and confusion surround enforced distribution of the wealth. It is hard to enforce something so unclear and subjective. Enforced equality fails on the human level; an equalitarian paradise could never transpire, because few could agree on what it is, or how to achieve it.

In society, wealth is increased when trade increases. Wealth is not increased when government demands more money from taxpayers. Government might redistribute wealth produced by others, but little of that wealth would reach the poor. As the saying goes, those who control the state usually enrich their friends.

POLITICS AND POVERTY

The libertarian alternative to poverty is also the most rational. As Rod Manis noted in the pamphlet, *Poverty: A Libertarian View,* "When power is radically decentralized, people will be free to run their own schools, their own welfare programs, their own lives.... The system that obtains the greatest individual freedom would be the most successful and would provide the greatest opportunities for the poor."

Freedom does not guarantee wealth or success; it guarantees only the individual's right to pursue them. Despite political promises of personal security from hunger and poverty, government cannot lessen the plight of the poor. Rather, the welfare state prolongs poverty and nurtures people's dependence on handouts. This is no accident. There is no better way to control members of society than to make them insecure and eager to accept any type of legislation in exchange for a so–called free lunch.

Poverty is nothing to look forward to. Yet it is not those countries with high levels of personal and economic liberties that suffer from mass poverty. The greatest resource of any nation is not iron ore, oil, or gold. It is the recognition, by members of that nation, of the individual's right to acquire personal wealth in liberty.

The question should not be, "What about the poor?"

The question should be, "What about the liberty not to be poor?"

The manager and co–manager of the Future of Freedom Conference series for five years in the 1980's, L.K. Samuels is a writer and libertarian activist. He founded Society for Libertarian Life (SLL) at the California State University, Fullerton in the early 1970's. He was instrumental in forming Rampart Institute, based on the works of Robert LeFevre. Former Northern Vice Chair of the Libertarian Party of California (2003-2007), he has authored a series of fiction and nonfiction books. Web site: www.Freedom1776.com. This article was published in the 1970s as a position paper for SLL

CHAPTER 15

YOU'VE SLID A LONG WAY, BABY!

By Wendy McElroy

The contemporary feminist movement is not an expression of individualism. The dominant viewpoint of mainstream feminism is political liberalism (in the modern sense of that term) with a strong socialist influence. The stress upon positive rights (the "right" to equal pay, the "right" to day–care centers) demonstrates the link between feminism and liberalism, while much of the rhetoric ("exploitation," "consciousness-raising") indicates its debt to socialism. It is not surprising, therefore, that women who uphold radical individualism are uncomfortable with the label of "feminist." The situation becomes puzzling, however, when one considers that the roots of American feminism were basically individualistic, and that much of the non–political feminist literature is highly individualistic in its call for the independent, liberated woman. This literature often stands in striking contrast to the political material, which demands collective, governmental solutions to women's problems.

Feminism, as an organized movement in America, is usually dated from the abolitionist movement of the 1830's—abolitionism being the radical branch of the anti-slavery movement, which insisted upon the immediate cessation of slavery on the grounds that every man is a self-owner. It was the first radical cause in America to encourage women as lecturers and writers; William Lloyd Garrison, in particular, insisted that he was fighting not for male rights, but for human rights. The clique of women who were strongly influenced by the anti–political, libertarian philosophy of Garrison formed the nucleus of the budding feminist movement.

Tracing the decline of individualism in America is a fascinating, albeit discouraging, process. The primary cause of its decline in the nineteenth century was the Civil War, which dealt a stunning blow to a young libertarian movement embodied in such figures as Josiah Warren, Lysander Spooner, William Lloyd Garrison, and Ezra Heywood. Feminism was among various social causes which responded to this shift toward statism by gradually altering their goals and strategies to accommodate, rather than to retard, the process. Although the bond between feminism and libertarianism was not broken, it was severely weakened. Today, the activities of nineteenth–century libertarian feminists are virtually ignored by the current movement, or, if mentioned, the ideology of the figures is conspicuously absent, even though the most minor socialists are repeatedly labeled as socialist. This Orwellian memory hole in the fabric of feminism exists despite the fact that the libertarians Moses Harman and Ezra Heywood were among the first to be arrested under the Comstock laws for distributing birth control information; Angela Heywood was virtually the only voice calling for legalized abortion in America in the 1890's; and Lillian Harman and E. C. Walker were one of the first couples to be imprisoned for violation of marriage statutes in America.

Undoubtedly, the prominence of socialism accounts for the bias with which histories of the feminist movement have been written. As libertarian ideas are aired and are applied to a widening range of social problems, a confrontation between socialist and individualist ideologies is bound to occur.

Feminism is based on the idea of women as a "class"—a class being defined as "a group of individuals classified according to common characteristics." The common characteristic is subjective, dictated by the purpose of the grouping. It could be eye color, income bracket, race, location, or religion. For a political theory, as feminism purports to be, the crucial question is: what characteristic explains something politically significant about the group? Is there something over and above the sexual characteristics of women which best explains the political problems confronting them?

This is the first point at which individualist feminism diverges from both mainstream and Marxist feminism. The notion of women as a distinct class presents a difficult problem for Marxists. Orthodox Marxism distinguishes classes solely according to economic criteria (the ownership of the means of production), not according to sexual characteristics. By this theory, women belong either to the exploited working class or to the exploiting ruling class; individual women can be laborers or capitalists. There is no unity provided by sharing a common sex. It is, therefore, difficult for Marxists to define women as a class.

Marxist feminists have offered different solutions to this dilemma.

The most popular of these solutions seems to be the postulating of a dual system: capitalism and patriarchy, viewed as separate systems which coexist and support each other. Thus, women can be categorized not only according to their economic status as workers, but also according to sex.

Mainstream feminism faces an equally perplexing situation. By demanding equal representation of women in politics, its proponents point to sex as the essential characteristic. But many women who have entered politics are notably conservative in their views, and oppose such popular feminist measures as abortion and the Equal Rights Amendment (E.R.A.). Is having these women in a position of power a victory or a setback for mainstream feminism? Is there a sense in which having in power a man who advocated abortion and the E.R.A. would be preferable to having a woman who opposed them?

If the stress is upon women as a sex, then the election of the most reactionary of women must be regarded as a triumph. If, however, liberal feminists condemn women with conservative positions, then ideas—principles, rather than sexual characteristics—are the defining common characteristics.

A key question is as follows: if the government were executing male dissidents, would feminists demand—in the name of equality—that an equal number of women be executed? In most cases, they would not. Thus, no matter what is being said, it is not merely a matter of equal treatment under the law. Underlying this or any theory of equality is a theory of rights, and of what rights can properly be enforced by government; otherwise, equality under reprehensible laws would be an acceptable goal. There is an implicit concept of "justice," which is the crux of the difference between individualist feminism, and liberal or Marxist feminism.

The libertarian theory of justice applies to all human beings, regardless of secondary characteristics such as sex or color. Every human being, simply by being a human being, is a self–owner, which means that every human being has moral jurisdiction over his or her own body. To the extent that laws infringe upon self–ownership, they are unjust. To the extent that such violation is based upon sex, there is room for a libertarian feminist movement. Women become a political class not due to their sexual characteristics, but because the government directs laws against them as a group. The political class "feminist women" has been created by the historical and current legal discrimination women have suffered from the state.

Although nearly every woman has experienced the uncomfortable and often painful discrimination which is a part of our culture, this is not a political matter. Peaceful discrimination is not a violation of rights. One of the risks of claiming autonomy is that you must extend this right to all other individuals, some of whom may deal with you in an offensive manner, or may refuse to deal with you at all.. The freedom of association requires the right to say "no" and to refuse association. Freedom of speech requires the right to be rude, biased, and wrong. As offensive as this behavior might be, it is not a violation of rights, and it is not a subject that libertarianism as a political philosophy addresses, except to state that all remedies for it must be peaceful.

Just as Marxist class analysis uses the relationship to the mode of production as its point of reference, libertarian class analysis employs the relationship to the political means as its standard. Society is divided into two classes: those who use the political means, which is force, to acquire wealth or power, and those who use the economic means, which requires voluntary interaction. The former is the ruling class which lives off the labor and wealth of the latter.

This form of class analysis leads to another major difference between individualist feminism and the liberal or Marxist variety. By rejecting the political ruling class, libertarian feminists are logically led to reject the political means of solving social problems—in particular, the problem of legal discrimination against women. Libertarian feminists cannot consistently condemn the ruling class as parasitical while they are trying to swell its ranks by attaining political power. Although occurrences of discrimination may always be on an individual level, it is only through the political means that such discrimination can be institutionalized and maintained by force. Given this context, individualist feminists must view the state with great suspicion, if not outright condemnation.

GOVERNMENT IS FORCE

Government is force. This is a moral, not a strategic point. The individualist–feminist Voltairine de Cleyre expressed her view of government as force:

> A body of voters cannot give into your charge any rights but their own. By no possible jugglery of logic can they delegate the exercise of any function which they themselves do not control. If any individual on earth has a right to delegate his powers to whomsoever he chooses, then every other individual has an equal right: and if each has an equal right, then none can choose an agent for another, without that other's consent. Therefore, if the power of government resides in the whole people and out of that whole all but one elected you as their agent, you would still have no authority whatever to act for that one.

Lysander Spooner, perhaps the foremost American theorist, echoed this sentiment in an article criticizing women's suffrage. It is extracted from Benjamin Tucker's *Liberty:*

> Women are human beings, and consequently

> have all the natural rights that any human
> being can have. They have just as good a right
> to make laws as men have, and no better; *and
> that is just no right at all.* No human being, nor
> any number of human beings, have any right to
> make laws, and compel other human beings to
> obey them. To say that they have is to say that
> they are the masters and owners of those of
> whom   they   require   such   obedience....
> [Emphasis in the original.]

Spooner concluded by stating:

> If the women, instead of petitioning to be
> admitted to a participation in the power of
> making more laws, will give notice to the pre-
> sent lawmakers that they are going up to the
> State House, and are going to throw all the
> existing statute books in the fire, they will do a
> very sensible thing.

The libertarian view of class, justice, and government is
in direct opposition to that of contemporary feminism. In
particular, the concept of justice is in conflict with the
liberal and Marxist demand for enforced socio–economic
equality. Libertarians insist that the freely chosen actions of
individuals be respected. This concept of justice is "means
oriented." As long as a given social state has resulted from
the voluntary interactions of everyone involved, it is just.
Justice, therefore, refers not to a specific end state, such as
equality, but to the process by which the end state is
achieved. If no rights are violated, justice is achieved.

This is not to say that an ideal, humanitarian society will
be the result. It is to say that the best we can do is respect
people's freedom. In contrast, the Marxist and liberal
feminists' conception of justice is "ends oriented." The end
is equality, or a classless state. Within this context, the
demand for socio–economic egalitarianism may be instituted by force.

The mainstream and Marxist feminists call upon the
state to protect women from the consequences of autonomy,
from the peaceful actions of others. Although the

relationship between an employer and employee is voluntary, the state is pressured to protect the interests of exploited women. Any coercive interference in a voluntary exchange—one undertaken for the benefit of one or both of the contracting parties, as opposed to the benefit of the aggressor—is paternalism. When the government discriminates in favor of any group on the grounds that the group is unable to take care of itself, the government is assuming the role of parent. Although paternalism is a doctrine most often applied to children and mental incompetents, it is now applied to women. Women are granted a legal overseer to monitor their interactions in order to prevent "exploitation." Feminism is the paternalism of our time.

THE NEW PURITANISM

Feminism is also the new puritanism. Coupling a demand for sexual freedom with a horror of publications such as *Playboy* or *Hustler,* many feminists attempt to stretch theories of exploitation and the demand for paternalism into sexual areas. Although it would be denied by the many *Playboy* centerfolds who flocked to interview for that well–paying position, many feminists hold that men's magazines exploit women because they contribute to the tendency to view women as sex objects. Such a tendency should be discouraged – so their argument goes -- by laws restricting how women may be presented. In their view, pornography is sin, and laws should promote virtue.

Paternalism often results in a form of puritanism, for in order to protect the interests of a particular group, the government must assess what is "good" or "bad" for that group. The good is institutionalized into society, while the bad is prohibited. In libertarian theory, however, laws protect rights instead of virtue, and the individual is free to be wrong. To deny this freedom is to take from women, and from men as well, the power of choice, in yet another area of their lives.

Abolitionist feminists struggled to increase choice by breaking social taboos and repealing discriminatory laws. It's sad that contemporary feminism has reversed the process and now calls for censorship and protective legislation. But with time and scholarship, perhaps a fine tradition can be redeemed.

A weekly columnist for FoxNews.com, Wendy McElroy is a Canadian individualist anarchist and individualist feminist. She is author of over a half–dozen books, including *Liberty for Women: Freedom and Feminism in the Twenty-First Century* (2002), *Freedom, Feminism, and the State* (1999), and *Debates of Liberty: An Overview of Individualist Anarchism, 1881–1908* (2003). She is a research fellow at the Independent Institute in Oakland, California. This essay is from *Caliber* (Summer, 1982). McElroy's web site is: www.WendyMcElroy.com.

CHAPTER 16

THE COUNTER–ECONOMY ALTERNATIVE

By Samuel Edward Konkin III

Libertarianism has matured as a full theory in philosophical, historical and anti–political fields. Based on a simple premise of non–aggression and appropriate self–defense (or none), it has developed to the extent of offering a fairly satisfactory criticism of most current ideologies and of the issues of modern statism. Since 1969, a movement has grown to the size where considerable division of labor is practiced; educational institutions and activist groups are staffed; and numerous periodicals, large and small, internal and external, are published.

Soon after this movement burgeoned, a vexing question emerged: how does one get there from here? There is a society based on the libertarian principle; here is your present situation. Even if the populace was educated, and theory further developed and passed on through more education, to what immediate ends would the educated act? Action against the State was carried out in political terms, but action for a free society was undefined and, hence, unclear.

Alternatives first offered fell into two basic options: participate in the present anti–libertarian mechanisms of the State (politics), or withdraw from not only the State, but from statist society. The first option led to compromise and co–opt; the second led to coral–reef utopian pipe dreams and nomadic, "drop–out" wandering, and social irrelevance.

The answer, or at least an answer, was discovered in 1973. Modern libertarianism is particularly concerned with economics. An understanding of the present economic system of various forms of State intervention—hereafter called Economics—was well developed, but the only practical alternative offered was not to act. Again, this limited analysis led to "working within the system" to restrain and reduce intervention—or to dodge it and await the millennium. The crucial problem was seen at this time as how to deal with (State) Economics and build a free society step by step.

Many people have successfully dealt with the Economics of the State for as long it has been around. During extreme, highly visible, state intervention—such as war–time controls, prohibitions, and sudden tax increases—black markets, "underground" economies, tax rebellions, and such emerged as popular movements. Investigation of these phenomena by advanced libertarians revealed startling and highly encouraging facts.

Counter–Economics was the rule, not the exception, throughout the highly statist parts of the world. Nalevo production and trade in Russia, "black labor" and goods in Europe and Latin America, smuggling, tax evasion, and forbidden immigration thrived, and in many cases, contributed the majority of the "national products."

Everywhere in relatively free North America, where the State intervened, the Counter–Economy responded. Trucking regulations generated evasions of speeding laws. Prohibition generated bootlegging, and drug controls generated dope–dealing. The State tried to control women's bodies: counter–economy feminists marketed contraband contraceptives and an underground midwife industry. Growing taxation generated forty million (by government estimates) tax evaders, innovating new techniques and business practices. Confiscation of wealth through money inflation generated alternative, mainly illegal, forms of money and even counter–economy banking.

Obviously, these counter–economists were, and are, practicing free–marketeers. Surprisingly, few had any grasp of libertarian theory. Lacking such a full understanding, their activities were limited to single industries and they often oppressed others. Gun–runners would oppose dope dealers; tax rebels would denounce alien smugglers;

feminists would recoil from gold–bugs and vice versa. Lacking a coherent ideology, the practicing counter-economists also warred internally, with ideas of "making their bundle and then going straight." Thus, rather than expanding their numbers within their field and linking with other types of counter–economists for trade and social intercourse, they stayed "in the closet" until they could "go straight."

This "guilt trip," or self–internalizing of statist pseudo-morality, prevents the Counter–Economy from replacing the Economy. As free–market ("Austrian") economics tells us, the free–er market—much more efficient, productive, and especially, innovative—will easily triumph over the controlled market. All that is lacking is the market demand for that victory.

This, then, is the role suitable for the libertarian activist. He and she become the entrepreneurs of liberty—selling the libertarian explanation and moral defense of the Counter-Economy, and destroying the statist mystique. They will increase its size, first, by encouraging counter–economists to use their techniques in other activities and exchanges in their lives; second, by encouraging and training new entrepreneurs into the Counter–Economy; third, by developing and extending the communications and information flow both internally and interfacing externally; and, fourth, by convincing libertarians to enter the Counter–Economy and to "practice what they preach"— becoming convincing examples.

A fully integrated Counter-Economic Libertarian is an agorist. Theory meets practice and the mind–body dichotomy is resolved. Many libertarian alternatives have been offered, and more will and should be developed. But it's hard to envision any libertarian strategy which does not at least include agorism and unleash the Counter-Economic alternative. For as the market goes Counter-Economic, the State starves for lack of taxes and wealth to control, and must die.

And is this not the Libertarian Revolution?

Samuel Edward Konkin III (1947–2004) was editor of New Libertarian. He was a strong opponent of party politics, including the Libertarian Party. He wrote *The New Libertarian Manifesto* (Anarchosamisdat Press, 1980; second printing by Koman Publishing Co., 1983). He founded the Movement of the Libertarian Left and The Agorist Institute.

CHAPTER 17

WHO'S AFRAID OF NO GOVERNMENT?

By L.K. Samuels

That government is best which governs not at all; and when men are prepared for it, that will be the kind of government which they will have.

–Henry David Thoreau, *Civil Disobedience*

Who's afraid of no government?

Apparently, most people are. But even if the thought of no government does not bring out gasps of fear, surely the mere utterance of the word "anarchist" will. After all, who condones chaos, violence, and terrorism? No one, of course. But few people understand that when it comes to chaos, violence, and terrorism, governments of the world have almost a monopoly. This is the important question: why is it that when a group of men, who have no nation–state, kill innocent people, the act is called "terrorism"; but when Israel, Jordon, France, or any other nation–state commits the same kind of acts—killing innocent people—it is called "defense"? Isn't terrorism still terrorism, no matter who commits it?

Governments are terrorists, but they hide their actions behind the label of nationalism and patriotism: war becomes defense; theft becomes "taxation"; slavery becomes "conscription"; terrorism becomes "defense." Few people question the violations; rather, if they do protest, it is because the government is oppressing the "wrong" group of people, and not because they regard coercion itself as wrong.

What, then, is *no government?* What is anarchy? *No government* is the absence of government. It is the absence of terrorism, chaos, wars, regulations, taxation, and military drafts. It is the absence of physical aggression upon another human being. This is why many people have turned against governments—because governments are the largest perpetrators of violence and terrorism.

If a self–avowed anarchist were to terrorize a community or injure people, he would be mimicking the actions of a government. If enough of these so–called anarchists were to organize and seize a country's government by force, they would become the new governmental leaders. How could these rebels be anarchists if they are *rulers* of a country?

They are not anarchists, of course. They are terrorists, underground politicians, would–be dictators, or aspiring military generals. Advocates of *no governmental coercion* have no interest in acting like rulers of nation–states. Again, if they were interested, they would not be anarchists.

Physical violence is the key. To employ initiated violence in order to eliminate government is to imitate government— to engage in political power plays, civil wars, and revolutions which serve only to replace one set of rulers with another. That is hardly in keeping with the ideal of *no government*.

It should be remembered that the nihilists of Russia, who were often labeled as "anarchists," were terrorists seeking to depose the Czar and to rule in his place. The nihilists were an underground government, employing the same kind of violence to topple the government as the government was employing to oppress the people and to destroy the nihilists. The nihilists were neither peaceful nor anarchistic.

THE LIBERTARIAN ANARCHIST

To differentiate themselves from other so–called anarchist factions, the term *libertarian anarchist* was coined. Similar to the individualist anarchist of the nineteenth century (and Professor Murray Rothbard's "anarcho–capitalist"), the libertarian anarchist comprises a small but important percentage of the general libertarian movement (around 25 to 35 percent).

The goal of the libertarian anarchist is to dismantle the *belief* that some overseer must rule, control, or dominate another human being. Note that the libertarian anarchist wants only to abolish the idea, willingness and allegiance of citizens to be victimized by government (a victimization more massive and destructive than could ever be accomplished by any band of terrorists). This is the battlefield.

The battle involves consistency and reason. People must discover that initiating violence does not solve problems; it creates them—whether committed by governments, service organizations, gangs, or individuals. Violence breeds violence. It is the catalyst for most rebels. Government aggressed upon them, and they feel compelled to strike back.

The libertarian anarchist first deals with increasing justice and decreasing aggression on the personal level, before hitting the big time with the atrocities of worldwide governments. After all, government action usually reflects the characteristics of its particular society. Therefore, the libertarian anarchist is not engaged in replacing one set of rulers with another—be they scoundrels, saints, or libertarians. It is impossible to halt aggression of governments or individuals by becoming part of it. Nor can the situation be changed by joining or competing with a system which legalizes coercion. If a group (*e.g.*, a political party) tries to join the system in the hope of eventually undoing the government's injustices, that group must also defend the very corrupt system that it is working to change. The result? The status quo. Rulers—not rulership—are replaced.

GUARDING INDIVIDUAL LIBERTY

People often fail to recognize that government is the worst possible vehicle to provide or guard the rights of life, liberty, or property. If a government is in a position to permit certain liberties by edict or legislative enactment, that government can dictate or legislate away such rights— and they will. Individual rights are not gifts of gods or governments; they are naturally born out of everyone's equal liberty to live peacefully, without perpetration of physical force or fraud against persons or property.

The main reason for government's constant violation of individual rights centers on the attitudes of the populace at large. People are often quite willing to disregard or violate their neighbors' rights. It is this attitude which is the root of government's ability to trespass on the rights of individuals.

Basically, it is natural for people to take advantage of others if given the opportunity, and government has been found to be the most effective and profitable means to accomplish this on a colossal, mass scale. In psychological terms, government represents the people's *id:* a malignant monster of the subconscious mind, which has been made respectable by sheer numbers of people, *i.e.*, majority rule.

Rulership by the masses is no virtue. The German voters brought the National Socialists and Hitler to power in the 1930's. The masses in the pre–Civil War South (United States) believed in the enslavement of blacks. In fact, during the 1850's, the U.S. Supreme Court upheld this enslavement. Just because the masses favor something, does not make it right.

After the Civil War, Congress did abolish one kind of slavery—the ownership of people by other people. But although *individuals* could no longer own people as chattel, Congress did not abolish other types of slavery: *government* was still permitted to own people. In other words, the masses—the public sector—could own individuals.

When the King's Court abolished slavery in England (1830's), the lawyers who opposed slavery argued that when a black slave entered England, he was obligated to serve just one master—the King of England—no one else. The argument won favor with the judges, and the court ruled that people residing in England were the king's subjects who owed allegiance to the crown alone, and not to any individual. In other words, the king is the universal slaveholder.

In the United States, government has replaced the monarchy as the universal slaveholder. The American black slave could have his allowance (if he had any) seized at any time. The slave's life could be taken by his overlord, and any small liberties granted by a slaveholder could be rescinded.

The modern–day citizen lives under similar conditions in that his allowance (income) is seized in taxes; his life is taken in wars; and his limited liberties are constantly rescinded by parliaments, dictators, or congresses. If a citizen refuses to pay taxes, government will seize his property and imprison him. Slavery is at issue here because the government claims that by refusing to pay taxes, the citizen has, in effect, stolen money from the government. Government thus maintains that it owns the total income of every citizen, and that it has graciously allowed citizens to keep some of their own money. The government owns the citizen, 100 percent.

THE UNNECESSARY EVIL

How can oppression be abolished without the dismantling of the entity which manufactures the oppression? It cannot. The best way to eliminate the oppression and corruption emanating from government is to eliminate—eventually—the need for government. If people begin to see government as it really is, and if they would refuse to cooperate or participate in government—through tax–evasion, draft–evasion, etc.—the State would crumble of its own weight.

It is disturbing to see that some people never learn from history.

Demands for stronger and stronger government to solve the problems of the nation–state are heard daily—the very problems caused by the State in the first place. Stronger government leads only to stronger possibilities of a larger, more corrupt State, capable of committing greater injury against individuals and minorities; and as the State grows in strength, the individual—as the overseer of his own life— grows weaker. It is inevitable. An authoritarian government cannot exist in an environment of strong, independent, free, and volitional people. As the saying goes: power corrupts; absolute power corrupts absolutely.

The best method to protect individual liberties is by *not* entrusting them to untrustworthy institutions. And what institution is *more* untrustworthy than the State? Think about Watergate, C.I.A. operations, secret campaign funding, Nixon's enemy list, I.R.S. harassment of the administration's enemies, C.I.A. assassination attempts, the Vietnam Conflict, secret files on political troublemakers, the Plumbers, etc.

Thomas Paine wrote, "Government is a necessary evil;" but Paine never foresaw the technology now available to government to commit such mass atrocities as those seen with the rise of national socialism (fascism) and international socialism (communism). Both ideologies reduce an individual's existence to the status of a national resource.

It is apparent that the crucial error of the early American revolutionaries' attitude was accepting the evils of government as necessary. Evil is never necessary. Evil can never be justified. Evil is evil. So government must be classified as an *Unnecessary Evil.* This is the major position of the libertarian anarchist whose tradition is embedded in the teachings of Thomas Jefferson and Thomas Paine. The libertarian anarchist refuses to support *any* inherently evil institution—especially the State.

Many argue that without a government, chaos and lawlessness would reign. Is it not possible that this is exactly what the State wants people to believe? Would State–owned and –controlled public education systems teach anything else? Would politicians preach anything else but that public pencil–pushers and agencies are indispensable?

BAREFOOT IN THE NETHERLANDS

When Professor John Hospers, of the U.S.C. Department of Philosophy, lectured in the Netherlands, some members of the audience became upset and confused with his stand against government–operated enterprises. They approached him after the lecture, and complained that they disliked walking barefoot. Dumbfounded, Hospers said he had never discussed that issue. An assistant from the Netherlands whispered to him that in his country, most shoes are manufactured by the government. Apparently, many in the audience thought that Hospers' opposition to nationalization would result in a shoeless Netherlands—as if only government could produce shoes.

People have been conditioned to believe that without government, even in certain areas, chaos and disorder would erupt. Nothing could be further from the truth. Under the First Amendment, government is forbidden to enter the field of free press or speech; therefore, press and speech exists in an environment of anarchy. Yet, where is the chaos?

Samuel L. Blumenfeld wrote: "Has history not shown that when governments are destroyed, people not only manage to survive, but the basic fabric of society is maintained? Does society not depend more on individual self–control for stability and prosperity than on government control?" (*Penthouse*; November, 1973)

Order, organization, and stability do not originate from government. As Robert LeFevre points out in *Does Government Protection Protect?* (1978), order originates from three areas: family, business, and fraternity. These areas represent the greatest involvement of peoples' lives. What else is there? And if someone becomes disorderly in an attempt to rob or murder another, protection—as a commodity—can be provided outside of government. Already, non–government fire departments (*e.g.*, Rural/Metro Fire Department, Inc. in Scottsdale, Arizona) and non–government policing businesses (see Chapters 7 and 12) are in operation. Furthermore, more than one million cases have been handled through private arbitration court systems in recent years. Even national defense could be provided by contributions from citizens, as well as policies from insurance agencies, all voluntarily.

Order is derived from free trade and trust, and there is nothing so chaotic and devious as governments involved in wars and oppression. Free individuals have little reason to be chaotic or rebellious. If no one has the authority to control the lives of other people, there is obviously no institution against which to rebel.

When a person is free to choose his lifestyle and run his own life, it is to his advantage to be orderly, especially in economic matters. In a free society, individuals would be too busy living life to engage in chaotic actions or to attempt control of another. Even if a person or –a group tried to impose control over others—without the legitimacy of a government—the cost would be prohibitive. Wars are expensive, and most people would view the plundering, would–be government as terrorists and thieves.

It was Johnny Carson on "The Tonight Show" who made an astute observation during President Gerald Ford's trip to Russia and Japan in 1974. At the time, a new vice president had yet to be approved by Congress. Commenting that without a vice president, "no one is running the country," Johnny then paused and asked, "Notice the difference?" He received thunderous applause from his audience.

THE PROPER FUNCTION OF GOVERNMENT

What is the proper function of government? In the Western world it is believed that the government's most important duty is to protect citizens from criminal elements: to prevent murder, theft, and injury. But these crimes are enforced only on an individual level. What of the State's legalization of such crimes? Aren't these violations of the proper function of a government in a free society?

Why is it possible for the State to murder and rob citizens, yet to prohibit private murder and robbery? Why is a citizen arrested and jailed if he attempts to "tax" or "draft" another? Isn't this a double standard? How can the State demand that people be honest and moral, when the State is neither? Moreover, isn't the government merely an association of individuals in the first place? If so, why should those in government have any more authority over life and death than the people in the streets? If the government is "the people," then, as "the people," why aren't they at the same level of authority as everyone else?

It should be noted that government is not physical. That is, government cannot be physically touched by human hands. Only individuals, who make up the governing body of the state, are physical in substance. Society and government are mere concepts, lacking material form. Unfortunately, many people place their faith, respect, patriotism, and obedience in an institution which, by conservative estimates, has resulted in the deaths of one billion men and women in countless wars, prison camps, torture chambers, inquisitions, imperialistic ventures, and so forth—from Stalin, Mao, Hitler, Attila the Hun, Napoleon, and Caesar, to thousands of lesser–known leaders who had the misfortune to rule in smaller, less powerful nations. In fact, Professor R. J. Rummel, author of *Death by Government*, estimates that 262 million citizens were murdered by their own government (democide) during the twentieth century alone.

Despite all the suffering caused by governments, despite all the killing *(e.g.,* 40 million people killed in World War I alone), and despite the billions of dollars' worth of property damage, many citizens are eager to follow the bidding of their government, although it has all the potential of reverting to past atrocities at almost any moment. This has been one of the oldest precepts of mankind: never question the existence of government; just question who should run it or how it should be operated.

THE HOME OF RATIONAL ANARCHISM

The traditional home of rational, peaceful anarchy is America.

Most of the frontier days were lived in an environment of anarchy or extremely limited statism. A number of early American colonies had large communities without taxation or government authority. In essence, they were living in *de facto* anarchy. If roads were needed, the community would assist with funding, voluntarily. If protection was needed, again, the community would provide it without coercion. The colonies had to provide their own services on a private basis. The English kings, for over 150 years, ignored the colonies, providing them with little funding to build roads, develop cities, or provide protection. Even during the American Revolution, the Continental Congress had *no authority* to tax or draft the American citizenry. It was all voluntary. (However, some individual American colonies did draft men to fight the British.)

In the tradition of Jefferson and Thoreau, the libertarian–individualist anarchist is opposed to all forms of aggression, and has nothing in common with the European socialist anarchist, who is often characterized as a black–capped bomb thrower. Nor is the libertarian anarchist happy with so–called libertarian anarchists who are supporters of the Libertarian Party. These "partyarchs" believe that some form of free society can be achieved through the political process.

Unfortunately, the word "anarchy" has a bad name, basically because of the stigma of the Eastern European socialist–anarchist. These pseudo–anarchists strongly believe in the initiation of violence. They have killed government officials, destroyed property, and have tried to raise armies—all of which are unacceptable to the libertarian anarchist. The pseudo–anarchists are no better than government. They are simply trying to assume the same old role of an almighty State. If anything is to be feared, it is violence of any means, initiated to justify someone's ends.

If violence is feared, so should government be feared. If chaos is feared, so should government be feared. Government—not the absence of it—should be feared.

The manager and co–manager of the Future of Freedom Conference series for five years in the 1980's, L.K. Samuels is a writer and libertarian activist. He founded Society for Libertarian Life (SLL) at the California State University, Fullerton in the early 1970's. He was instrumental in forming Rampart Institute, based on the works of Robert LeFevre. Former Northern Vice Chair of the Libertarian Party of California (2003-2007), he has authored a series of fiction and nonfiction books. Web site: www.Freedom1776.com. This article was published in the 1970s as a position paper for SLL

CHAPTER 18

THE
THOUSAND-YEAR WAR

By Richard J. Maybury

The research for this special report was begun in August, 1981, just after the air battle in which two Libyan jets were shot down over the Gulf of Sidra. I believed the research was complete in September, when I wrote, "The ouster of the Shah of Iran, the embassy crisis and the Gulf of Sidra incident are only the beginning. The violence will continue to escalate." The final draft was being typed when Anwar Sadat was killed.

Upon hearing of the assassination, I scrapped that draft, and resumed my research to try to discover what the next incident would be. The revised draft, contained herein, was finished and distributed just a few days before news of the Libyan hit squads sent to kill President Reagan appeared in the headlines.

The situation described in this report is not hopeless, despite the fact that nuclear weapons are involved. It is, however, caused by a near–total disregard for the principles on which America was founded, and it will continue to deteriorate until these principles are revived.

December 12, 1981

Failing to understand the history of the Holy Land, the U.S. government may have already entered World War III. But there is still time to make peace.

The murder of Anwar Sadat and the August air battle between U.S. and Libyan jets have again riveted our attention on the Mideast and the Arab–Israeli war. How and when did all this violence begin? Who is in the right, and when will the bloodshed end?

The answers lie far back in history. During the 5th and 6th centuries, the Roman Empire was not only disintegrating, it was also at war with the Persian Empire. This constant turmoil reduced the legal system of the Mediterranean world to a confused, cancerous growth, riddled with contradictions, and changing whenever the political wind changed—which was frequently. This caused large portions of the Mediterranean economy to be badly disorganized, producing widespread poverty. The Dark Ages were beginning.

A well–traveled, highly intelligent businessman, known to his associates as "The Trustworthy One," decided something had to be done. To straighten out the law, he reasoned, it would be necessary to revive the old biblical idea that a Higher Authority than man's governments is the source of an individual's legal rights. (Twelve centuries later, Thomas Jefferson's Declaration of Independence would repeat this idea by saying all men "are endowed by their Creator with certain unalienable rights.")

To accomplish this legal reform, the businessman—Mohammed—created a new religion, Moslemism, which quickly became popular among Arab peoples living around the Mediterranean. As planned, the legal reforms this new religion produced enabled the people to organize their economic activity in a more rational manner. The Arab–Moslem Golden Age was born, and prosperity became widespread. Moslemism, or Islam, became the dominant religion in the Mideast, but not everyone converted. Many Jews and Christians kept their religions, so the whole area became a religious melting pot, something like America today. Europe, on the other hand, accepted neither Islam nor any other system of legal reform; so the European economy remained disorganized, and the people lived in the squalor of the Dark Ages instead of the prosperity of a Golden Age.

THE HOLOCAUST

Then in 1000 A.D., Pope Silvester II laid the plans for one of the most savage persecutions in history. A century later, his plans were carried out as Pope Urban's Crusaders swept down out of Europe to "liberate" the Holy Land from the Saracen "infidels," and establish European–style governments there. In this barbaric effort to forcibly remove the Moslems from their Mideast homeland, wave after wave of Europeans rolled through the Moslem civilization in a hurricane of death, torture, and destruction lasting two centuries.

Cities were leveled. Thousands of men, women, and children were tortured and murdered, and large land areas were depopulated. The two–year siege of Acre alone killed 100,000 people—the same death toll as that resulting from the atomic bomb that was later dropped on Hiroshima. At Jerusalem, the Archbishop of Tyre declared, "The city presented a spectacle of such slaughter of enemies and shedding of blood that it struck the conquerors themselves with horror and disgust."

Not satisfied with butchering children, babies, and the aged, the Crusaders went on to kill pets, livestock, and zoo animals. When 10,000 terrified, helpless Moslems took refuge in the Mosque of Soliman, all were slaughtered. The dismembered bodies were then removed, the pools of blood mopped up, and the mosque converted into a church dedicated to the Prince of Peace.

When the Crusaders arrived in Egypt, the Moslem city of Damietta was a thriving commercial center inhabited by 70,000 prosperous individuals. When the Crusaders left, Damietta was a ruin haunted by 3,000 sick and starving wretches. It was eventually abandoned.

The desert encroached on once–fertile farmland, as the most advanced civilization seen on earth up to that time was ravaged. The progress of all mankind was retarded. There's no telling what kind of prosperity we'd be enjoying today if the Arab–Moslem Golden Age—with its emphasis on science, math, and technology—had not been brutalized by the Crusaders.

But the holocaust of death and destruction did not end with the Crusades. It merely evolved into the Inquisition which continued to rob, torture, and murder Moslems until Napoleon finally halted it in 1808. The Moslems have never forgotten it. Many of them still think "Christian devil" is one word.

DEMOCRACY VS. LIBERTY

Along the eastern Mediterranean seaboard, the area known as Palestine—part of which would later be renamed Israel—became a poverty–stricken no man's land. By 1500 A.D., it had been so devastated by war and desert encroachment that its population was declining. Governments could collect little or no tax from it, so it was mostly ignored by them. The governments that did rule it made only half–hearted attempts.

Indeed, political apathy was so great in Palestine that many individuals could choose the legal system to which they would adhere. In any given community, it was not unusual to find Moslems living under Islamic law, Christians living under Christian law, and Jews living under Jewish law. Since all the legal systems agreed in their basic principles—don't kill, don't steal, etc.—rarely did followers of a legal system try to force their law onto someone else.

The important point here is that during the long period between the Crusades and this century, the various faiths in Palestine got along rather well together. Having little government, they had no major wars. Their few clashes were nothing compared to the massive battles of today. Mostly the Moslems and Jews left each other alone.

Then in World War I, the Turkish and British governments turned the Holy Land into a battleground, and many Arab Moslems sided with Britain's "Lawrence of Arabia." At the cost of many Arab lives, T.E. Lawrence brought Palestine under British rule; and the British continued the custom of benign neglect—at first. Moslems and Jews lived peacefully, but then the British government decided to turn humanitarian. It began working to create a "Jewish National Home" for European Jews settling in Palestine. This British favoritism toward the Jews caused resentment among the Moslems, who remembered the Crusades and Inquisition. They feared that someday a government of European Jews would arise in Palestine, just as governments of European Christians had arisen centuries earlier.

Following a 1929 riot between Moslems and Jews, a British commission of inquiry found, "The Arabs have come to see in Jewish immigration not only a menace to their livelihoods but a possible overlord of the future" [emphasis added]. Nevertheless, in 1937 the do–gooder British government suggested Palestine be partitioned, with Arabs from the Israeli sector being forcibly removed from their homeland.

The British had revived Pope Silvester's plan.

Then the World War II Nazi persecutions of the Jews caused a massive influx of Jews into Palestine, thereby frightening the Arabs even more. Finally, the British government realized it had created a time bomb, but instead of defusing the bomb by backing away from the creation of a "Jewish National Home," it decided to cut and run. In 1948 it fled Palestine, leaving the country virtually free, with no government at all.

That's when the time bomb exploded. The Jewish immigrants had brought with them political beliefs which held democracy to be more important than liberty. And not only did they believe in majority rule, but they were new to Israel and had very little understanding of Moslem history. Now comprising an Israeli majority, they decided they were entitled to put their democratic beliefs into practice. Some of the more farsighted Jews warned against it, but they, like their Arab Moslem neighbors, were overwhelmed by the majority.

When the British left, the Jewish majority instantly set up a Jewish government, and proceeded to impose taxes and laws on everyone—Moslems and Jews alike. Thus they not only threw away their newfound liberty, but they also completely ignored James Madison's famous warning made in 1787:

> *Hence it is that such democracies have ever been spectacles of turbulence and contention; have ever been found incompatible with personal security or the rights of property; and have in*

*general been as short in their lives as they have
been violent in their deaths.*

Suppose you were an Arab Moslem dedicated to your
religious heritage and mindful of the Crusades and
Inquisition, and you heard Israeli Prime Minister Menachem
Begin's statement, "This is a Jewish state which we want to
have a Jewish character."[1] How would you react? Would
you pay taxes to support the Jewish state? Would you obey
the Jewish state's laws? Or would you fight?

TANK BATTLES AND TERRORISM

The Arabs remember the old Christian Crusades, and
they are so enraged over this new Jewish Crusade—called
Zionism—that their judgment is warped (note that Zionism
is a political movement intended to build the Jewish
government in Israel; some Jews are Zionists, others are
not).

A rational defense against the Zionist government's taxes
and controls merely would have required the Arabs to follow
the example laid down by our own Sons of Liberty in the
1765 Stamp Act rebellion. First, they should have informed
the Jewish government that it was welcome to enact all the
laws it wanted, as long as it didn't try to impose them on
Moslems. Then they should have formed local, independent
militias, and paid peaceful but armed midnight visits to any
bureaucrat foolish enough to enforce the Jewish laws. This
would have triggered mass resignations among the Jewish
bureaucrats, just as it did among the King's bureaucrats in
1765.

There was no need to confront the Jewish government's
military forces. Ambushing a bureaucrat here and there is
the most it ever takes to make enforcement of taxes and
controls very lax. A favorite tactic of the Sons of Liberty was
to post notices around a bureaucrat's home warning that
anyone who was vigilant in the enforcement of the law
would have an "accident."

Using this strategy, the Arabs would have remained free
even though living in the midst of a Jewish government.
Their situation would have been something like that of
Tennessee bootleggers who pay little tax on their liquor
because their rifles make revenue agents reluctant to find
them. After all, what bureaucrat is going to risk getting shot
just for a measly civil service pay check?

Instead, however, the Arabs are so paranoid from

centuries of persecution that they've overreacted. Forming their own government, the Palestine Liberation Organization (P.L.O.), they've levied taxes and controls on themselves and tried to wipe out the Jewish government.

Imagine what would happen if American bootleggers formed a Tennessee Liberation Organization for the purpose of wiping out the American government. Their farms would be obliterated by paratroopers on search–and–destroy missions; their skies would be darkened by helicopter gunships; and their mountain roads would be clogged with tanks. They would never be free.

Neither will the Arabs. Having their own government, they are experiencing all the miseries accompanying government. Instead of a few Arab militiamen using ten-cent bullets to shoot an occasional bureaucrat, as Tennessee bootleggers do, the Palestinian Arabs have allied themselves with other Arab governments, and gone head to head against the Israeli government in massive tank and air battles.

In short, the Arabs aren't fighting for liberty; they're fighting for victory.

The P.L.O. is little different from any other government; it believes that the end justifies the means. So it condones terrorism. Many of its fiery members think that killing innocent Jewish children is O.K., reasoning that if the children aren't killed, they'll grow up to continue the persecution begun a thousand years ago. The P.L.O. also assumes that two wrongs make a right. Each time a Jewish child is killed, it points to the Jews who, in the process of setting up their majority rule in 1948, found it "necessary" to wipe out an entire Arab village.

When the sword is once drawn, the passions of men observe no bounds of moderation.

Alexander Hamilton, 1787

THE SPIRIT OF THE CRUSADES

As far as the Arabs are concerned, the Arab–Israeli war is merely the latest episode in the Crusades and Inquisition that began during the Middle Ages. As the Moslem rector of al–Azhar University in Cairo once said, "We religious leaders have also to make clear to the Islamic peoples that the lingering spirit of the past Crusades that was utterly routed by the feats of valor and heroic resistance of our forefathers has made of the present–day Zionism a spearhead launched against Muslims by the enemies of humanity and advocates of imperialism..."[2]

By "enemies of humanity and advocates of imperialism," he meant the United States. The U.S. alliance with the Israeli government aggravates the Mideast situation terribly, because America is a predominately Christian nation. To the Arabs, we are the descendants of the Crusaders and Inquisitors; and by siding with the Israeli government we have confirmed all the Arabs' worst fears. They now believe America, the most powerful nation ever seen on earth, is helping the Zionists continue the thousand year persecution. This has frightened millions of them so badly that an American has become to them what a Nazi is to a Jew—we are "the great Satan." P.L.O. chief Vasser Arafat: "We face the huge, barbaric American and Israeli powers, but we are with the current of history."

Incidentally, this brings up the reason the Russian government cannot subdue Afghanistan. Russia too is predominantly Christian, and the Soviet government pursues an atheist policy; so the Moslem guerillas in Afghanistan are not fighting a political or economic war, they are fighting a jihad—a holy war. They are called mujahidin (holy warriors) because they are fighting against the Soviet Crusaders, for Allah.

THE SHORES OF TRIPOLI

In 1948, the Moslems' hatred and fear of Americans was, however, not new. It was merely a re–awakening of feelings dormant for more than a century—feelings stemming directly from the Inquisition. These feelings are what the phrase in the Marine Corps hymn, "from the halls of Montezuma to the shores of Tripoli," is all about; and they make the August air battle between U.S. and Libyan jets very important.

Look at a map and you'll find the air battle happened over the Gulf of Sidra near Tripoli. These are waters claimed by Moslem rulers since the 1500's.

In those days, many Moslems living in the Barbary States of North Africa were refugees from the Inquisition, and they were levying a tax on Christian vessels sailing along the African coast. Christian merchants somehow convinced their governments to pay the tax for them, so the Moslems knew they could make the tax quite hefty.

Resentful of the Inquisition, the Moslems raised the tax frequently, just as they raise the price of oil today. Finally, in 1801 the tiny American government could no longer afford to pay the tax. But U.S. merchantmen continued sailing through the area anyhow, so the pasha of Tripoli captured and imprisoned the tax evaders. The U.S. replied by invading North Africa, bombarding Tripoli and forcing the pasha to back down.

The U.S. saw the incident as a victory. But the Moslems saw it as a revival of the Crusades, and they behaved accordingly. At every opportunity, they raided American ships sailing in the Mediterranean.

Not understanding the Moslem assumption that the Crusades had been revived, the Americans called the Moslems "pirates"; and in 1815, marines led by Commodore Stephen Decatur were dispatched to teach the "pirates" another lesson. They succeeded, and many Moslems have been bitter toward America ever since. (They haven't felt too friendly toward any western nation. They fought the French in Algeria in 1850, and at Khartoum in 1885, threw the British entirely out of the Sudan, killing British hero General Gordon in the process.)

American history books refer to those battles as the Barbary Wars.

But the Moslems simply consider them to be "Christian America's" contribution to the Crusades. Islamic rulers still regard the southern Mediterranean as their own, and any American use of these waters can rub salt in a very deep, old wound.

Therefore, when the U.S. fleet was deliberately sent into that specific area[3] in 1981, the Libyans could hardly have seen the maneuver as anything except a revival of the 1815 conflict—a revival of the Crusades. Christians versus Moslems.

That is why the air battle came as no surprise to the Reagan administration. A thousand years of history indicated it was as good as inevitable. (Not to mention the fact that the Libyans made more than 40 attempts to warn the U.S. jets away before they finally got fed up and attacked.[4]) Those were not American jets fighting Libyan jets, they were Crusader jets fighting mujahidin jets.

This means the Gulf of Sidra incident was highly significant, because it was "Christian America's" first intentional combat role in the Arab–Israeli war. I repeat: America has entered the Arab–Israeli war. Millions of Moslems now regard us as battlefield allies of the Israeli government. We are at war with Islam.

NO DEFENSE

Hopefully Libya's Colonel Muammar Abu Minyar al-Gaddafi and his allies will cool their terrorist activity now that they've been given a bloody nose by the U.S. fleet. But a thousand years of history say they won't. As the deputy prime minister of Turkey once said, "NATO, the Common Market and the West in general are inspired by the spirit of the Crusades"[5]; and as Ayatollah Khomeini once said, "The U.S. does not seem to realize that it is fighting Allah."[6]

We are only kidding ourselves if we think the Moslems will back down. Their ancestors didn't run from King Richard's knights, and they won't run from us. Further, their numbers are growing so rapidly that soon there will be a thousand million of them, well equipped with arms and oil money, scattered from Morocco to Indonesia. Gaddafi: "We are the doormat of the world, but we shall change that!"

It is very possible the P.L.O., the Moslem Brotherhood, and their allies will now see us as legitimate targets for atrocities like the 1972 massacre at the Munich Olympics. In fact, the recent escalation of terrorist attacks on U.S. military and diplomatic personnel in Europe may be the beginning of the Moslem counterattack. The Gulf of Sidra incident may well turn out to be the new Gulf of Tonkin incident. But with a difference: after the Gulf of Tonkin incident, the North Vietnamese had no ability to retaliate against the U.S. mainland. The Arab Moslems may not be so helpless.

There now exist, stored in armories around the world, thousands of U.S., Soviet, British, French, and other tactical nuclear weapons small enough to be hidden in suitcases. While the large strategic nuclear weapon gets all the publicity, it is the small tactical weapon which is the most serious threat to us and our families.

No security system is foolproof. Not ours, not the Soviets', not anyone's. Therefore it can only be a matter of time till a Moslem mujahidin finds a way to steal a few bombs—assuming none has been stolen already. Dozens could be carried off by one person driving a pickup truck. One of the more common types, so compact it can be fired from an 8-inch gun, will produce a blast, fireball, and mushroom cloud of fallout sufficient to kill most of the people in downtown San Francisco...or Dallas...or Tulsa...or Anchorage...or...[7]

Our nuclear retaliatory ability is not a defense against this. In fact, there is no defense. As Albert Einstein warned, "There is no defense in science against the weapons which can now destroy civilization."

The Moslem holy warriors often act independently of any government—their first loyalty is to their God, not their nation—just as Sirhan Sirhan acted independently when he shot Robert Kennedy. If (when?) a bomb is set off, we probably won't even know who did it. Will it be someone from Libya? From Iran? Pakistan? All we will know for sure is that thousands of us will have died because the government that represents us angered someone. (As thousands of innocent men, women, and children died at Hiroshima because the government that represented them had attacked Pearl Harbor.)

A key point here is that the Holy Land is sacred to Moslems as well as to Jews and Christians. So a Moslem mujahidin is much more likely to plant his bombs in the U.S. than in Israel.

Nevertheless, at the Gulf of Sidra, Uncle Sam rejoined Pope Silvester's Crusades. I hope it doesn't cost us any cities.

G.I. JOE: HOLY WARRIOR

The creation of the Israeli government severely radicalized the entire Moslem world, but the radicalization is not uniform. In every Islamic country, there is strong disagreement over the methods for dealing with this reincarnation of the old Crusader governments. (Emphasis

on the Israeli government, not the Israeli people. Most
Moslems still direct their feelings toward the Zionist state,
not the Jewish people. However, the longer the war drags
on, the more this distinction becomes blurred, and the more
innocent Jewish civilians are murdered.)

Numerous Islamic political groups vie for control of their
nations, and Moslem tempers run very hot. Execution and
assassination are often seen as legitimate parts of the
political process, because many Arabs believe the danger
from the Crusaders is so grave that drastic action is
needed. In the city of Beirut alone, there are 45 different
independent armed brigades,[8] each with its own viewpoint
on the Israeli government.

The ouster of the Shah of Iran and the murder of Sadat
are only the beginning. As long as the Israeli government
exists in its present form, this type of violence will continue
to escalate; mujahidin versus mujahidin. So every Islamic
government frantically seeks powerful allies to help protect
it.

Some Islamic governments seek help from the United
States. Egypt and Saudi Arabia are examples. Others seek
aid from the Soviets. Libya and Syria for instance. Please
note, however, it is the Islamic governments that are siding
with the U.S. or Soviet Union, not the Islamic people.

Allegedly in exchange for guaranteed oil deliveries,
President Reagan declared for the first time on October 1,
1981, "I have to say that Saudi Arabia, we won't permit to
be an Iran;" and he pledged U.S. military aid for the
protection of the Saudi government from all threats,
internal as well as external.[9]

This makes it a lead–pipe cinch that American troops will
indeed be sent to Saudi Arabia, just as they were sent to
Vietnam in the 1960's. Many Saudi Moslems will be
enraged, understandably, at their government's alliance
with the "Christian devil" Americans, and they will escalate
their overthrow attempts. In short, America's promise to
intervene will create the need for the intervention!

Most American servicemen are of Christian and other
non–Moslem faiths. I wonder what their reactions would be
if they understood they are now the Saudi government's

holy warriors, committed to fight and perhaps die in a Moslem religious conflict.

ASSASSINATING TRAITORS

"Let there be no more bloodshed between Arabs and Israelis."

Those are the words of the late Anwar Sadat, and they are the reason he was killed. When Americans heard those words they heard, "Let there be no more Mideast violence. Let the oil flow freely. Let there be peace."

But millions of Moslems heard, "Let there be no more defense against the Zionist Crusaders who invaded our homeland. Let the Jewish government keep what our ancestors died for, and let the thousand–year persecution be successful. Let us surrender, and forsake our religion."

American rulers are fond of referring to Mideast allies such as Sadat, the Shah of Iran, and the Saudis as "moderates." They refer to Khomeini, Gaddafi, and others who oppose the "moderates" as "Moslem fundamentalist extremists"—as members of the lunatic fringe. But the opposite is true.

The Shah was overthrown; Sadat was killed; and the Saudi rulers fear a similar fate, because they are the fringe group. In the intensely religious Moslem nations, they are the extremists. As one P.L.O. official said, they are "outcasts in the Arab world."

As long as the Israeli government continues repeating the mistakes of its Crusader predecessors, tens of millions of Moslems will regard any Moslem who speaks of peace as a traitor. This is why the death of Sadat was followed not by widespread demonstrations of mourning, but by widespread celebrations.

It is also why the Reagan administration's well–publicized wish to "do something" about Gaddafi is very risky. Many Arab Moslems consider Gaddafi to be the new Saladin—the man who can eject the Zionist government from Palestine just as the original Saladin ejected the Crusader governments. If some well–intentioned, patriotic

American accepts the Reagan administration's suggestion and makes a martyr of this Saladin....

THE GREAT SNAFU

How much actual discrimination against Arab Moslems exists in Israel? The Israelis claim it is minimal, and my research reveals little reason to disagree. I doubt it is as bad as the discrimination against blacks in the U.S. [This was written in 1981. –Editor]

But the actual discrimination now existing in Israel is virtually irrelevant. What counts is what the Arabs think exists.

Having fled Israel years ago, thousands of Arabs now live in refugee camps outside Israel, where they cannot be discriminated against; and because of past injustices, real or imagined, they are afraid to go back. They just sit and wait, and hope for the day when it will be safe to go home.

This gruesome situation is caused by the fact that the Jews will not give up their claim that Israel is a "Jewish national home," even though they cannot clearly define it. What is a "Jewish national home," and are the Jews being realistic when they expect Moslems to obey its laws and pay its taxes?

Every time a Moslem refugee hears "Jewish national home," his belief is reinforced that he will be discriminated against if he were to return to Israel.

Very likely the single biggest snafu in the history of the Holy Land was the public relations snafu the Jews committed when they named their country and described it as a "Jewish national home." Instead of calling it "Israel," they should have chosen a secular name with no religious undertones—something as simple as "New Palestine" would have been fine—and described it not as a "Jewish national home" but as a "place where Jews could always be free."

The Israelis, however, are not alone in their sloppy use of language.

The Arabs constantly refer to their desire to "utterly destroy the Zionist state of Israel." What does this mean?

The Jews think the Arabs want to follow Hitler's example and kill every Jewish man, woman, and child in Israel. This is why swastikas are seen occasionally in cartoons depicting Arabs. But the vast majority of Arabs want only to dismantle the Jewish government. Thus the Jews believe they are defending their families against another Nazi–type holocaust, while the Arabs believe the Jews are defending the Jewish government.

To "utterly destroy the Zionist state of Israel" is to awaken Jewish memories of Nazi persecution. And to establish a "Jewish national home" in the Holy Land is to awaken Moslem memories of the Crusaders' persecution. Neither side seems to have any sympathy or interest in the other's heritage. Both prefer to shoot first and ask questions later. So the two most persecuted peoples in the history of mankind · are now persecuting each other.

PUSHING THE AMERICAN "HOT BUTTON"

By now you're probably saying the Mideast is such a hopeless mess, such a cesspool of paranoia, terror, and persecution, why did the U.S. ever get involved? Why did our rulers ally themselves with the Israeli, Egyptian, Iranian, and Saudi rulers?

To defend someone's liberty? I doubt it. In fact, I doubt there are a dozen people in the entire Mideast who know anything about liberty. They've shown no signs of interest in the principles of 1776, and they certainly haven't been practicing the tolerance which their religions claim is the first step toward liberty. (Perhaps the clearest lesson history teaches is that you can't have liberty, or the prosperity that accompanies it, unless you understand and apply the principles that make it possible.)

So was it oil? I doubt that too. Neither Israel nor Egypt has much oil, and the U.S. was involved in the Mideast right from the beginning in 1948, long before the energy crisis.

More likely, it was the fact that the creation of the Israeli government triggered an arms race between Jews and Arabs. Both sides wanted money and weapons, which means they both needed a rich uncle to subsidize them. The two richest uncles in the world are Uncle Sam and Uncle Ivan—the U.S. and the U.S.S.R.

But no rich uncle will part with his money unless he has a good reason. So it is necessary to find his "hot button" and push it, and push it, and push it.

Uncle Sam's hot button is the "Soviet communist threat." Uncle Ivan's hot button is the "American capitalist threat." The Israeli government discovered it could trigger an avalanche of U.S. money and weapons into its coffers if it

said it opposed the "Soviet communist threat." The Arab
governments found they would be similarly supplied with
Soviet money and weapons if they said they opposed the
"American capitalist threat."

Over the years, governments throughout the world have
pushed these buttons with spectacular success. Dictators
on both sides in Korea and Vietnam pushed them with
great glee. But the Israeli and Arab governments deserve
the credit for discovering them.

The absurdity of all this is magnified by the fact that very
few people in the Mideast know or care anything about
communism, capitalism, or any other economic or political
philosophy. What they know and care about is religion.
(That's the people who care about religion. The
governments, like all governments, care about power.) The
Mideast war is not a battle between communists and
capitalists. It is a battle between Crusaders and Saracens.
Those people think in terms of Bible and Koran—Moses and
Mohammed—not Karl Marx, Adam Smith, or the
Communist Manifesto.

Like the Korean and Vietnamese rulers, every Mideast
ruler uses Uncle Sam and Uncle Ivan in every way they can.
Sometimes Sam and Ivan are used as sugar daddies.
Sometimes they are used as bogeymen. But make no
mistake about it—they are being used.

That's why Egyptian rulers, to cite one example, saw no
problem in switching their loyalty in 1973 from the Soviets
to the Americans. It makes no difference to them whether
they oppose the "American capitalist threat" or the "Soviet
communist threat." They don't care, as long as they keep
getting the money and weapons necessary to increase their
power.

Saudi Crown Prince Fahd: "There are many states such
as the Soviet Union which are only too ready to supply the
kingdom with everything it wants. In other words, we could
easily replace the Americans."[10]

You and I, like the Jewish and Moslem peoples of the
Mideast, are being hoodwinked by the power-hungry Jewish
and Moslem governments.

HOW WILL IT END?

Jews and Moslems lived peacefully, side by side in

Palestine for centuries. But now, both have powerful governments, and they are paying the inevitable price. As Thomas Paine said in 1792: "...man, were he not corrupted by governments, is naturally the friend of man,... human nature is not of itself vicious."

The Arab–Israeli war—the Moslem–Zionist war—will never end unless the Jews start believing in liberty rather than democracy. As long as there is majority rule in Israel, the Arabs will continue defending their religion; which means that in their paranoid state, they'll continue murdering innocent Israeli children. (Which is why the Israelis, too, are acquiring atomic weapons. Arafat claims, "They have 23 to 25 nuclear bombs."[11] He doesn't say whether they built them or stole them.)

Consider: if you were one of the millions of Moslems friendly to both the Afghan and P.L.O. causes, would you not love to see the Soviet and American governments blast each other off the face of the earth? If you could get your hands on a truckload of A–bombs, would you not be tempted to blow up several Soviet and American cities, hoping the two superpowers would retaliate against each other?

How do we know A–bombs are not being stolen and planted right now? Would any government admit some of its bombs are missing? Is it not possible that the murder of Sadat and other recent terrorist attacks are just diversions to draw our attention away from the real Moslem offense now being prepared?

Does anyone seriously believe the descendants of the great warrior Saladin, who threw the Crusaders out of Jerusalem eight centuries ago, will be content merely to commit assassinations and fight border skirmishes?

Lest anyone think I exaggerate the western governments' habit of wantonly and sadistically goading the Arab Moslems into war, I offer this anecdote. During World War I, the French government won control of Syria, and in 1920 sent General Henri Gouraud to act as governor there. Upon entering Damascus, Gouraud walked up to the tomb of Saladin, knocked on the door, and gloatingly announced, "Saladin, listen: we have returned."[12] The Moslem uprisings against the Christian French lasted two decades, and today Syria is one of the most militant Islamic nations. If Paris vanishes in a ball of fire, you can bet the battle cry of the terrorist who does it will be, "Remember Gouraud!" But have the French ever apologized to the Syrians? Has any western government ever apologized to any Moslem for anything?

One person with two suitcases could incinerate both

Washington, D.C. and Moscow.

The stage was set a thousand years ago, and all sides are morally wrong. The Israeli government's cause is wrong; the Arab government's tactics are wrong; and the western and Soviet governments' interventions are wrong. Perhaps the Holy Land, where nuclear weapons are now accumulating, is where man will soon face the most severe ultimatum of his million–year evolution: either learn to exist without government, or cease to exist.

SOLUTION: LIBERTY

World War III has already started. It began in 1948 with the creation of the Israeli government, and it is a religious war. We entered it at the Gulf of Sidra, and it will continue to escalate until nuclear weapons are detonated, perhaps in our homeland.

It was the intention of Jefferson, Madison, and the other Founding Fathers that when the federal government finally grew powerful enough to threaten the security of the nation, the state and local governments would rise up to stop it. That time has now come. In order to protect our cities from acts of nuclear terrorism invited by the federal government's Mideast interventions, every governor, state legislator, and local official should now demand adoption of the following plan. The plan is based on the principles of 1776—Common Law, Higher Authority, and Natural Rights. These are, after all, universal principles which can yield liberty and prosperity whenever they are applied.

1. The U.S. government should sever all ties with all Islamic governments immediately. (See George Washington's Farewell Address, 1796.)

2. The U.S. government should sever all ties with the Israeli government unless the Israeli government adopts total religious freedom. This means:

A. Any person, of any religious persuasion, may come and go in the Holy Land as he or she pleases, subject only to those laws on which all major religions agree. These are laws against theft and violence, and laws which preserve contracts. In Thomas Jefferson's words, "The interests of society require the observation of those moral precepts only in which all religions agree (for all forbid us to murder, steal, plunder, or bear false witness)...." These laws will number so few that soon after they are enacted, there will be no further work required of the Israeli legislature, and all legal matters can be handled by the Israeli courts using the procedures of the old Common Law.

B. The only taxes to be collected in the Holy Land are those necessary for peace officers and courts to enforce the above laws.

C. No one is to have an automatic "right" to any service, subsidy or other assistance from the Israeli government, except the peace officers and courts for which he is paying taxes. If schools, hospitals, welfare, military defense, or other public services are desired, supporters of the Jewish government or members of other religious or nonreligious groups are free to create their own agencies to produce these services, provided they do not force their projects onto persons who do not share their beliefs.

D. The Israeli government will abandon its attempt to develop a legal definition of "Jew," and will remove any references to race or religion from all of its laws. Wherever possible, all government–owned real estate will be returned to the individual Palestinians from whom it was taken, and the remaining government real estate will be sold or homesteaded to any private individual, regardless of race or religion. (Real estate now privately held will not be affected.)

This plan does not ask the Israeli government to do anything it shouldn't have done right from the very beginning—namely, apply the principles of liberty. In fact, the plan's emphasis on voluntary, rather than coercive, public services is exactly the direction the Jews were originally headed before the British government's do–gooder humanitarians started getting people killed.

If the plan, or one similar to it, is not adopted soon—or if it fails—there surely will be enough atomic bombs, owned by enough Moslem holy warriors, that our cities will be in grave peril. In that case, the U.S. government must withdraw completely from the Mideast and declare absolute neutrality. It will not even be able to encourage or prohibit private sales of arms to the Mideast, because any intervention of any kind will make someone angry. It must remain totally aloof to the Mideast—in George Washington's words, "detached and distant." (Incidentally, if the Soviets fail to disengage from the Mideast, they too will stand a good chance of losing a few cities).

Otherwise, I can't see how the state and local governments will have any choice but to secede from the union. The only way they will be able to save our homeland will be to announce that the federal government no longer represents anyone except itself—the states accept no responsibility for its mistakes. I would expect Texas and Alaska to be the first to secede, since they have plenty of oil, and therefore no reason to allow their cities to remain imperiled.

A final point: the Arab–Moslems know that the U.S. is the main source of public and private aid to Israel. So some of them undoubtedly believe that if they can trigger a war between America and Russia, they will not only divert Russian pressure away from Afghanistan, but they will also reduce American aid to Israel, thereby making Israel more vulnerable to invasion. In short, a plan for total religious freedom in the Holy Land is as essential to the Israelis' survival as it is to ours. If we are bombed, Israel will be on its own.

There is still time to stop World War III, if we act now.

Formerly the Global Affairs editor of *MoneyWorld*, Richard Maybury has written more than 20 books and monographs on topics ranging from monetary policy, geopolitics, and investments to foreign policy in the Middle East and the former Soviet Union. Two of his most popular books are *What Ever Happened to Penny Candy?* and *The Thousand Year War in the Middle East*. Founder of Henry Madison Research, Inc., he is considered one of the top business analysts in America. Web site: www.Chaostan.com.

[1] "Behind the Concerns about Israelis New Government," *World Business Weekly*, 24 August 1981, 11.

[2] John Laffin, *The Danger of Islam* (Bantam Books, 1981), 58.

[3] Walter S. Mossberg, "U.S. Downs Libyan Jet...." *Wall Street Journal*, 20 August 1981, 3.

[4] Mossberg, ibid., and "Washington Whispers," *U.S. News and World Report*, 31 August 1981, 12.

[5] Laffin, ibid., 136.

[6] Ibid., 178.

[7] Nigel Calder, Nuclear Nightmares (Viking Press, 1979), 28 and Robert Heinlein, *Expanded Universe* (Ace Books, 1980), 491.

[8] John Weisman, "Why the Palestinians are Losing the Propaganda War," *TV Guide*, 2 October 1981, 11.

[9] Gerald F. Sieb, "Reason Asserts U.S. Will Defend Saudi Arabia," *Wall Street Journal*, 21 October 1981, 22.

[10] J.B. Kelly, "The Arming of Saudi Arabia," *Wall Street Journal*, 12 November 1981, 27.

[11] David Ignatius, "Yasser Arafat: Peace Prospects Poor," *Wall Street Journal*, 12 November 1981, 27.

[12] G.H. Jansen, *Militant Islam* (Harper and Rowe, 1979), 66.

CHAPTER 19

ROBIN HOOD
SELLS OUT!

By David Friedman

Ask not what the government can do for you.
Ask what the government is doing to you.

Although they agree that private property and the free market are ideal institutions for allowing each person to pursue his own ends with his own resources, many people reject complete laissez–faire, because they believe that it leads to an unjust, or at least undesirable, distribution of wealth and income. They concede that the market responds to the demands of consumers, expressed by their willingness to pay for what they want, in a much more sensitive and efficient fashion than that of the political system responding to the demands of voters, expressed by their votes. But they claim that the market is "undemocratic," because the number of "votes"—that is, the number of dollars available to be spent—varies widely from person to person. Therefore, they argue, the government should intervene in the market to redistribute wealth and income.

This argument correctly regards the free market as having its own internal logic, producing results, such as an unequal distribution of income, independent of the desires of its supporters. It incorrectly treats the political process as though it had no corresponding internal logic of its own. The argument simply assumes that political institutions can be set up to produce any desired outcome.

Suppose that one hundred years ago, someone had tried to persuade me that democratic institutions could be used to transfer money from the bulk of the population to the poor. I could have made the following reply: "The poor, whom you wish to help, are many times outnumbered by the rest of the population, from whom you intend to take the money to help them. If the non–poor are not generous enough to give money to the poor voluntarily, through private charity, what makes you think they will be such fools as to vote to force themselves to give it?"

One hundred years ago, that would have been a crushing argument.

Today it is not. Why? Because people today believe that our present society is a living refutation of the argument; that our government effectively transfers considerable amounts of money from the not–poor to the poor.

That is an illusion. There are some government programs that give money to the poor—Aid to Families With Dependent Children, for instance. But such programs are vastly outweighed by those having the opposite effect— programs that injure the poor for the benefit of the not- poor. Almost surely, the poor would be better off if both the benefits that they now receive, and the taxes—direct and indirect—that they now pay, were abolished. Let us consider some examples.

Social Security is by all odds the largest welfare–type program in America; its annual payments are about four times those of all other welfare programs combined. It is financed by a regressive tax—about ten percent on all income up to $7,800, and nothing thereafter. Those who have incomes of less than $7,800, and consequently pay a lower amount per year, later will receive lower payments, but the reduction in benefits is less than proportional. If the schedule of taxes and payments were the only relevant consideration, Social Security would be redistributing slightly, from higher–income to lower–income people.

But two additional factors almost certainly reverse the effect. Most Social Security payments take the form of an annuity—a certain amount per year, starting at a specified age (usually 65) and continuing until death. The total amount an individual will receive depends on how long he lives beyond age 65. All other factors being equal, a man who lives to age seventy–one will receive 20 percent more than a man who lives to age 70. Further, the amount an in- dividual pays for Social Security depends not only on how much he pays in taxes each year, but on how many years he pays. A man who starts work at age 24 will pay Social Security taxes for 41 years; one who starts work at age 18 will pay for 47 years. The first, other factors being equal, will pay about 15 percent less than the second, for 47 years. The first, other factors being equal, will pay about 15 percent less than the second for the same benefits. The missed payments come at the beginning of his career; since early payments have more time to accumulate interest than later ones, the effective saving is even greater. Assuming an interest rate of five percent, the accumulated value of the first man's payments, by age 65, would be about two–thirds as much as the accumulated value of the second man's payments.

People with higher incomes have a longer life expectancy. The children of the middle and upper classes start work later—often substantially later—than the children of the lower classes. Both of these facts tend to make Social Security a much better deal for the not–poor than for the poor. As far as I know, nobody has ever done a careful actuarial analysis of all such effects; thus one can only make approximate estimates.

Compare someone who goes to school for two years after graduating from college and lives to age 72, with someone who starts work at age 18 and dies at age 70. Adding the one–third savings on payments to the 30 percent gain in receipts (here the interest effect works in the opposite direction, since the extra payments for the longer life come at the end), I estimate that the first individual gets, from these effects, about twice as much for his money as the second. I do not know of any effects in the opposite direction large enough to cancel this out.

Social Security is by no means the only large government program that takes from the poor to give to the not–poor. A second example is the farm program. Since it consists largely of government actions to hold up the price of crops, it is paid for not only via taxes, but also in the form of higher food prices. Several years ago, when I did calculations on part of the Agriculture Department's activities, I estimated, using Agriculture Department figures, that higher food prices made up about two–thirds of the total cost of the part of the farm program I was studying. Higher food prices have the effect of a highly regressive tax, since poorer people spend a larger proportion of their income on food.

Higher prices benefit farmers in proportion to how much they sell; the large farmer gets a proportionately higher benefit than the small farmer. In addition, the large farmer can better afford the legal costs of getting the maximum benefit from other parts of the program. Notoriously, every year, a considerable number of farms or "farm corporations" receive more than $100,000 apiece, and a few receive more than $1 million in benefits from a program set up supposedly to help poor farmers.

So the farm program consists of a slightly progressive benefit (one which benefits those with higher incomes) financed by a regressive tax (one which taxes those with higher incomes somewhat less than proportionately to those incomes). Presumably it has the net effect of transferring money from the more poor to the less poor—a curious way of helping the poor. Here again, I know of no precise calculations that have measured the overall effect.

One could list pages and pages of similar programs. State universities, for instance, subsidizing much of the schooling of the upper classes with money from relatively poor taxpayers. Urban renewal uses the power of the government to prevent slums from spreading, a process sometimes referred to as "preventing urban blight." For middle–class people on the border of low–income areas, this is valuable protection. But "urban blight" is precisely the process by which more housing becomes available to low–income people. The supporters of urban renewal claim that they are improving the housing of the poor. In the Hyde Park area of Chicago, where I lived for many years, they tore down old, low–rent apartment houses and replaced them with $30,000 and $40,000 town houses. A great improvement for those poor who happened to have $30,000. And this is the rule, not the exception, as Martin Anderson showed, years ago, in The Federal Bulldozer.

This is not to deny that poor people receive some benefit from some government programs. Everyone gets some benefit from some government programs. The political system is itself a sort of marketplace. Anyone with something to bid—votes, money, labor—can get a special favor, but that favor comes at the expense of someone else. Elsewhere I argue that, on net, very nearly everyone loses. Whether or not that is the case for everyone, it surely is the case for the poor, who bring less to the bidding than anyone else.

A leading figure in the anarcho–capitalist community, David D. Friedman teaches law and economics at Santa Clara University. He holds a PhD. in physics from the University of Chicago, and he has written a series of books: *Price Theory* (1986), *Law's Order* (1999) and *Hidden Order: The Economics of Everyday Life* (1996). This essay is from a chapter in his first book, *The Machinery of Freedom* (1973).

CHAPTER 20

THE NON–AGGRESSION PRINCIPLE:

Treating Government like the Mafia's Grossly Retarded Big Brother

By L.K. Samuels

> *The Libertarian creed rests upon one central axiom: that no man or group of men may aggress against the person or property of anyone else. This may be called the "nonaggression axiom." "Aggression" is defined as the initiation of the use or threat of physical violence against the person or property of anyone else. Aggression is therefore synonymous with invasion.*

–Professor Murray N. Rothbard
For A New Liberty: the Libertarian Manifesto

Besides the self–ownership and free choice axioms, the Non–Aggression Principle is the linchpin of the philosophy known as libertarianism. As an ethical system for freedom, justice and prosperity, the Non–Aggression Principle simply states that "no one shall initiate the use of force or the threat of force." This means that violence should never be employed against peaceful individual(s), however, peaceful individual(s) have the option to use force in self–defense.

The Non–Aggression Principle is applied to all human behavior. It prohibits murder, rape, battery, kidnapping, robbery, enslavement, torture, and fraud. Libertarians see all aggressors, including governments, as bullies. To the libertarian, if it is wrong for an individual to commit violent crimes against another, the same restriction must be applied to the conduct of governments. If the average man in the street is prohibited from murdering and stealing, why should government possess some special legal right to commit these crimes?

If someone takes your property without permission, it is theft, regardless of how the money is used, or who committed the violent act. Nor does it matter how many people are involved in the violent act. Theft is theft, no matter if it is perpetrated by one robber or one thousand thugs. The injured individual is still victimized, no matter if it is inflicted by street gangs—the Bloods, the Crips, the Mafia—or by the Internal Revenue Service.

It is improper for governments in a free society to be the initiators of force and violence. The American founders explicitly established a very limited government. They wanted to prevent government from imposing coercive dictates and controls over its citizens. They visualized government as an impartial referee, to protect individual rights from bullies, criminals, and cheaters—not as the major player.

The Non–Aggression Principle is perhaps one of the most important ethical ideologies to arrive in the latter half of the twentieth century. Time will tell whether governments will stop acting like dogs marking coveted new territories, and start behaving in a peaceful, civilized manner.

The manager and co–manager of the Future of Freedom Conference series for five years in the 1980's, L.K. Samuels is a writer and libertarian activist. He founded Society for Libertarian Life (SLL) at the California State University, Fullerton in the early 1970's. He was instrumental in forming Rampart Institute, based on the works of Robert LeFevre. Former Northern Vice Chair of the Libertarian Party of California (2003-2007), he has authored a series of fiction and nonfiction books. Web site: www.Freedom1776.com. This article was written in 2005 for the Libertarian Party of Monterey County.

CHAPTER 21

WHAT IS LIBERTARIANISM?

By Martin Masse

What do libertarians believe in? In a few words, they believe that individual freedom is the fundamental value that must underlie all social relations, economic exchanges, and the political system. They believe that voluntary cooperation between individuals in a free market is always preferable to coercion exerted by the state. They believe that the role of the state is not to pursue goals in the name of the community. The state is not there to redistribute wealth, "promote" culture, "support" the agricultural sector, or "help" small firms, but should limit itself to the protection of individual rights, and let citizens pursue their own goals in a peaceful way.

Essentially, libertarians preach freedom in all fields, including the right to do what one wants with one's own body insofar as one does not infringe on the property and equal freedom of others. Accordingly, they believe that people who want to take drugs, watch pornography, prostitute themselves, pay for the services of a prostitute, or engage in whatever kind of consensual activity, should be able to do so without being importuned by the law and harassed by the police.

However, as libertarians—that is, notwithstanding their own personal preferences—they no more advocate a libertine way of life than any other, and one should not confuse the two words. What they say is that each and every person must be free to choose their own beliefs and the way of life that is appropriate to him or her, be it asceticism or libertinage, religious moralism or moral relativism. Libertarians will defend the right of the libertine to live in debauchery as well as that of religious fundamentalist parents to educate their children in accordance with their own very strict beliefs.

Libertarians support the formal equality of each and all before the law, but they worry little about the inequalities between rich and poor, inequalities which are inevitable and can be reduced only by encroaching on personal freedom and by reducing overall prosperity. To them, the best way to fight poverty is to guarantee a system of free enterprise and free trade, and to let private charity initiatives, which are more effective and better justified morally than state programs of wealth transfer, come to the rescue of those in need.

Libertarians believe that the only way to ensure the maintenance of personal freedom is to guarantee the inviolability of private property, and to limit as much as possible the size of the government and the scope of its interventions. They do not trust the state—whose managers claim to act in the name of abstract collective interests—when it comes to protecting individual liberty. According to collectivist ideologies, a viable social and economic order can be imposed and maintained only by the state. On the contrary, libertarian scholars have shown that it is the decentralized actions of individuals who pursue their own ends in a free market, which makes it possible to create and maintain this spontaneous order, to bring prosperity, and to support the complex civilization in which we live.

Thus, libertarians reject the main political development of the twentieth century, that is, the sustained growth in the size of the state and the range of its interventions in the private lives of citizens. To take one striking example, in 1926, public expenditures as a percentage of Canada's gross national product amounted to only 15%; by 2006, that figure had grown to 46%.

LIBERTARIANISM VS. CONSERVATIVISM

Within the North American political framework of the period after World War II, libertarians have allied themselves with conservatives in their fight against communism and socialism. This is why many people tend to confuse both philosophies and to put them on the right-hand side of the political spectrum, following the confused model of right vs. left, which is still widely used to categorize political ideologies. But libertarians are opposed to conservatives on several points, in particular on social issues, where conservatives often try to impose their traditional values on all by using the coercive power of the state when, for example, they support making drugs and prostitution illegal, or when they advocate official discrimination against homosexuals. On issues related to defense and foreign relations, conservatives are inclined to support militarism and imperialist interventions abroad, while libertarians advocate, when possible, isolationism and non–involvement in foreign conflicts.

In fact, conservatives value authority in itself and do not oppose state power in principle, doing so only when its aims are not the same as theirs. On the contrary, libertarians reject any form of government intervention. Many of them think they do not qualify as right–wingers and that the right–left spectrum should be replaced by another one which would place the statists and authoritarians of both left and right on one side, and the supporters of personal freedom of the other.

Libertarians are opposed to collectivist ideologies of all types, be they of the left or of the right, which stress the primacy of the group: nation, social class, sexual or ethnic group, religious or language community, etc. They oppose all whose purpose it is to regiment individuals in the pursuit of collective goals. They do not deny the relevance of these collective identities, but claim that it is up to the individuals themselves to determine which groups they wish to belong and contribute to. It is not for the state, or for institutions that derive their power from the state, to impose their own objectives in a bureaucratic and coercive manner.

In the ongoing debate over Québec's "national question," for example, most libertarians reject the independence project because its primary aim is to impose a Québec state which will be stronger, more interventionist, and more repressive toward those who do not fit the nationalist definition of Québécois identity. This being said, libertarians are not enthusiastic federalist patriots either, and they reject Canadian nationalism and protectionism in the same way, as well as the interventionism and administrative tyranny of the federal government. They do not see why they should choose between two states that infringe on our freedom more or less equally. Rather, they would want to see both federal and provincial governments reduced in size as much as possible.

AN HEIR TO CLASSICAL LIBERALISM

Although it remains relatively little known and little understood today, because of the near total submission throughout the twentieth century of Western intellectual life to collectivist thinking, libertarian philosophy is not a weird, marginal philosophy, propagated only by a small group of utopians disconnected from reality. On the contrary, it is heir to the most important Western political and economic school of the last centuries, classical liberalism, a philosophy elaborated by thinkers such as John Locke and Adam Smith. Beginning in the seventeenth century, it is the liberals who fought for a widening of political, economic, and social freedoms, against the power of the monarchs and the privileges of the aristocrats. Liberal principles are at the root of the American Constitution, and one can say that the United States as well as Great Britain and Canada were largely governed in a liberal way throughout the nineteenth century and up to the beginning of the twentieth.

Libertarian scholars have shown that it is the decentralized actions of individuals who pursue their own ends in a free market which make it possible to create and maintain this spontaneous order, to bring prosperity, and to support the complex civilization in which we live.

Then, why not use the word "liberal" instead of "libertarian"? Because the term "liberal," at the end of the nineteenth century, took on new meanings which are not at all compatible with the defense of individual freedom. In Great Britain, in Canada and in Québec, supposedly liberal parties are in fact only a little more moderate than avowed socialists in their inclination to use state power, and in their lack of respect for individual rights.

Worse still, in the United States, a liberal is a left–winger who advocates wealth redistribution and supports a big government that interferes everywhere in people's lives, one which tries to solve all real and imaginary problems by taxing and spending, and which creates bureaucratic programs for each good cause. In short, today's liberalism aims at creating a tyrannical state that does not hesitate to trample on individual freedom in the name of an unattainable collectivist utopia. This type of liberalism has nothing to do with classical liberalism.

Today's libertarians are inspired by former periods of liberal progress, but, after one century during which collectivist and totalitarian ideologies have dominated, they realize that classical liberalism was not strong or principled enough to stem the rising tide of statism. They are more coherent, or, some may say, radical, than traditional liberals in their defense of personal freedom and the market economy, and in their opposition to state power.

A PLURALISTIC MOVEMENT

Like all philosophical movements, libertarianism is varied, containing several schools and subgroups, and one will find no unanimity about its theoretical justifications, its goals, or the strategy it should adopt to reach them. In North America, a majority of those who call themselves libertarians would like to see the state brought back to a few essential functions: in particular, defense, foreign relations, justice, the protection of private property and individual rights, and some other minor responsibilities. All remaining functions should be privatized. In the context of a very decentralized federal state, libertarians accept however that local authorities (constituent states, provinces, regions, or municipalities) can intervene in other fields and offer various types of social and economic arrangements, insofar as dissatisfied citizens can easily move to other jurisdictions.

Some libertarians of the "anarcho–capitalist" school advocate the complete disappearance of the state, and the privatization of even the basic functions mentioned above. This goal may appear extreme or ridiculous at first sight, but it is based on a theoretically plausible argument. For example, it is easy to imagine that one could replace provincial, state, or municipal police forces (and the corruption, abuses of power, incompetence, and favoritism which usually characterize them) with private security agencies. These would make profits only insofar as they really protect citizens and fight real criminals. Anarcho–capitalists use the same type of arguments to support the privatization of the army and the courts, which would leave nothing for a state to do. Private firms would then provide all the services individuals might need.

In a context where public spending now accounts for almost half of all that is produced, where governments continue to adopt law after law so as to increase their control over our lives, a more realistic libertarian goal is simply to reverse this trend, and to fight for any practical advancement of freedom and any concrete reduction in state tyranny.

Libertarians are the only ones willing to enter this fight without compromising their beliefs. The fact is that the current ideological debate remains dominated by statists, despite the superficial political controversies that attract media attention.

On one side, socialists and leftist supporters of unlimited growth in the size of government make up a strong majority among lobbies feeding at the public trough, in universities and in the media. Most of what passes for journalism or academic research shows a complete lack of understanding of the basic rules of a market economy. In the "center," those who claim to be "realistic" admit that the state cannot continue to increase the tax burden and grow indefinitely, but they simply preach a slowing down of this growth. For its part, the business establishment would be satisfied with some minor cuts here and there, and few of its members question the corporatist structure of the state. As for those on the right who are described as radical "neo-conservatives," their stated aim is to take us back to where we were 20 or 30 years ago, when the ratio of state expenditures to GDP was five or ten percentage points smaller. That would be a step in the right direction, but hardly sufficient.

Also, one has to admit that the so-called "conservative revolutions" of the past 20 years in Britain, Canada, and the United States have not really produced major change, although some useful economic reforms and tax cuts were implemented. Few programs and laws were abolished, and the state still occupies a dominant place in economic and social life. It is even to be feared that bureaucratic programs will start growing again, now that budget deficits have been eliminated and governments have surplus revenues to spend.

Libertarians are the only ones who demand and work for radical change, a drastic reduction of the size and role of the state; they are the only ones who value individual freedom above all else. More and more people realize that libertarianism constitutes the only alternative. The libertarian movement hardly existed in the 1960's, and really took off in the United States in the early 1970's. The U.S. Libertarian Party, founded in 1971, is now third in importance after the Republicans and the Democrats. Whereas collectivist philosophies and Keynesian economics used to dominate academic life, recently there has been a revival of interest in classical liberalism and free market economics in the universities. Finally, today, libertarian philosophy can be found everywhere on the Internet, and its influence is growing in every continent.

Thus we can hope realistically that a century after the eclipse of classical liberalism, its libertarian offspring will once again become an influential philosophical doctrine and movement in the twenty-first century.

Martin Masse is director of publications at the Montreal Economic Institute. He is also publisher of the Canada-based libertarian webzine, Le Québécois Libre , which he founded in 1998. This essay was first published there on October 28, 2000. Website is www.QuebecoisLibre.org.

CHAPTER 22

IRAQ AND THE ROOTS OF WAR

By L. K. Samuels

March 19 marked the fourth anniversary of the invasion of Iraq by U.S. forces. Across California and the United States, thousands of demonstrators mourned this event with peace rallies, funeral marches, and speeches. Like many concerned citizens, I organized and participated in several peace rallies in the Monterey area. These rallies represented a wide coalition of groups and ideas, ranging from labor activists, Democrats, Quakers, and United Nations associations to libertarians. But when I delved deeper into why my fellow peace activists were protesting, I discovered that they know little about the causes of war.

The war in Iraq is no different from most wars, except that it has striking similarities to the Napoleonic wars. Fought across continental Europe in the early 1800s, these series of wars were allegedly fought to liberate the people from their oppressors. Napoleon repeatedly cited his intentions to replace kings and the nobility with liberty, equality, and fraternity. There was only one problem. The people in adjacent foreign lands did not want to be liberated and referred to the invading Napoleon as the bogeyman. The only revolutionary idea that Napoleon gave to Europe was adding propaganda to the arsenal of war.

The Bush administration is chanting the same mantra in Iraq, arguing that American troops are there to secure a stable democracy. Like Napoleon's forces, American troops are involved in nation-building to "liberate" the Iraqis and provide them with the tools of democracy, even though Iraq has never had a democratic government in its 7,000-year history, or possessed any grassroot movements advancing the concept of liberty.

So what is the root cause of war? Some sociologists point to the authoritarian attitudes of those who believe they are right, everyone else is wrong, and everyone must do as they command. This rigid mindset of one's own moral superiority permits ruling systems to engage in armed conflicts around the world and to commit all sorts of atrocities. Of course, any resulting collateral damage is considered acceptable because the war is being waged for a good cause.

Most wars are an affront to individual rights. When the few can command the many to do their murderous bidding, small conflicts tend to magnify into large ones. The concentration of power provides authorities with the collective means to execute their do-good pet policies. That is because most world leaders have succumbed to the Machiavellian notion that "the ends justify the means," contending that any violent act—murder, robbery, and so forth—is permissible providing that the end goal is a "greater good." And under this greater-good nostrum, the public often accepts the government's argument that war is peace, that freedom is slavery, and that invading a foreign nation with a preemptive strike is a defense maneuver.

As Randolph Bourne wrote in 1918, "War is the health of the state." Government thrives off war and the hysteria it spawns. Without such conflicts, the authorities could not justify increased spying on citizens and suspension of citizens' rights. Government needs war the way a heroin addict needs drugs. They need it to justify increasing taxes and expanding debt and to inflame nationalistic fervor. Governments need foreign devils and unstable conditions to prop up sagging popularity and economic policies at home. Even Thomas Paine recognized this truism in The Rights of Man, writing that "taxes were not raised to carry on wars, but that wars were raised to carry on taxes."

But the true culprit for war is a staunch belief in the infallibility of governmental power. To accept the legitimacy of the state is to embrace the necessity for war. For thousands of years, governments have been the quintessential war machine. If given the means, they tirelessly prepare for armed conflict with foreign and domestic opponents. They seek to protect their status, their authority, and their right to rule over others, creating an US versus THEM environment.

Conflict and war are the greatest threat to human liberty, life, and property. And a policy of perpetual war and nation-building eventually turns peaceful republics into violent empires.

The best road to peace is to allow citizens to structure their own lives as they see fit. When citizens are denied freedom, conflict flares and war is not far behind. Only a small, unobtrusive government can reduce intra-societal and foreign conflict. Only an open society, in which citizens freely choose their own personal and economic lifestyles, can ensure a peaceful way of life.

This article was produced for the Monterey County Libertarians for Peace, which L.K. Samuels co-chaired with David R. Henderson, and was later expanded into a newspaper op-ed piece for Libertarian Perspective in March of 2007. The national organization Libertarians for Peace is located in Washington D.C. under the leadership of anti-war activist Carol Moore (www.libertarians4peace.net).

CHAPTER 23

WAR IS SOCIALISM

By Mark Selzer

Socialism is an attempt by government, using physical force, to remake society to conform to a predetermined ideal. Whether the ideal is fairness, safety, equality, security, or stability, socialists seek to forcibly change society; war and endless conflict accelerate this process.

This process is most visible in foreign wars. The invading governments often have failed to deliver the utopia promised within their own borders, and they hope that war will provide more opportunity to use force to "fix" everything and create the ideal society. War confers vast political and military power on frustrated leaders who claim they are powerless to get things done or to perform promised reforms without it. For the socialist, left– or right–wing, Republican or Democrat, liberal or conservative, and all shades between, that is what makes socialism a war of perpetual conflict.

Conflicts often lead to war, since attempts to "fix" society usually fail to produce the desired results. The promised utopia never materializes. But this failure gives socialists an excuse to wage war on every sector of society, across neighboring nations, and even within their own ranks.

For instance, not only was Pol Pot's communist regime in Cambodia responsible for the deaths of millions of his own citizens, but his administration went after their own young cadres. When the socialist re-engineering of Cambodian society proved uneven, Pol Pot started a systematic purge of his own ranks—as had Stalin and Hitler with theirs—arranging the deaths of the "hidden enemies, burrowing from within." It has been estimated that up to 200,000 Khmer Rouge cadres were executed. Even in nations where the socialists failed to take over the government, the communists orchestrated their own self–destructive purges. When the Philippines' Communist Party began to lose influence after the 1986 removal of President Marcos, the Marxists blamed the Party's failures on their own members, killing some 2,000.

Instruments of war and conflict provide socialists with greater opportunities to justify using physical force to fulfill their dreams of universal equality or "fairness." But forcing people to accomplish certain objectives rarely works, so socialists, authoritarians, and governments are given a never–ending justification to demand more government interference in citizens' lives. In this way, warring against people is simply a systemic means to concentrate power, which in turn creates more conflict and chaos, as citizens resist. Caught in a cycle of incessant conflict, power addicts now have a continuous supply of excuses to boost their ego and authority. In such an environment, war and conflict become permanent fixtures of society. For socialists, therein lies the seduction of war.

WAR IS DESTRUCTIVE TO THE ECONOMY

Karl Marx argued that the best way to destroy market–based capitalism is through taxation. Money must be redistributed to fit the government's agenda. Obviously, communism and socialism cannot allow individuals to control their own financial destiny. However, both modern-day liberals and conservatives in the United States have wholeheartedly accepted this creed. Traditionally the nay-sayers to taxation, many right–wing conservatives, under the second Bush administration, have become cheerleaders for expensive wars and foreign adventures. In the past, the Democrats were the prime adulators for interfering in the lives of citizens in other nations as well as their own. But the fact remains that no matter who initiates war, the results are the same. Not only do wars destroy cities and lives, they also devastate the economy and those who support open marketplaces.

Since wars are financed by taxation and deficit spending, they remove resources from the economy that could instead generate resources for people to better their lives. For instance, each M1A2 Abrams tank costs over $4 million.

Add fuel costs, ammunition, training, maintenance, and a crew, and who knows how many additional millions must be taken from taxpayers and the economy? Further, war equipment is often operated to destroy or block economic activity, along with much of a country's infrastructure. Eventually, military equipment becomes damaged or outdated, and ends up as scrap metal or sold to some tin-pot dictatorship. This is a horrible drain on any country. War has a short productivity trail, because it does not produce profit or resources that can be used for the betterment of people's lives. It also creates a deflation in the economy that bears a deficit from the lost resources of war.

In contrast, consumer goods leave a more productive trail. For instance, the resources used to build computers provide additional resources for consumers down the line. With computers, new companies are able to be more productive and profitable, which in turn enables creation of more jobs and opportunities. This provides value, education, and cooperation, as well as a means for businesses to produce more housing, food, and a better quality of life.

WAR OFTEN FAILS,
LIKE MOST GOVERNMENT PROGRAMS

Wars have always been a popular means to raise taxes and grow government, as with any domestic government program. This is not to disagree with the stated goals of government, but to observe the apparatus of war, and to illustrate its similarity to welfare, rent control, social security, the "war" on drugs, or any other government application. To travel down this path and examine these facts, it is important to take a detached look at the stated goals of any government program. Whether they are palatable or not, the inner workings of a welfare/warfare apparatus must be examined dispassionately.

For the most part, libertarians do not disagree with the stated objectives "of government" to increase the welfare of the unfortunate. Who can argue with well-intentioned proposals to help the poor, defend our country, bring affordable healthcare to all, or protect neighborhoods from crime and pollution? The objection is not with such lofty ideals, but whether or not government should be the one that pursues them. Will forcing people to take particular actions in society end hunger and poverty? Or will that threat of force instead increase conflict, embitterment, and corruption? After all, very few of government's proposed programs have ever reached any level of success. Poverty has not been eliminated; affordable healthcare has not been provided to all; crime is still rampant in most parts of the world; and countries throughout the world are routinely attacked by other countries. After the expenditure of trillions of dollars to end poverty in United States since the 1960's, why is the poverty level now higher?

Anyone who visits the city of Watts, California, or any inner city ghetto, can witness the shabby result of 40 years and billions of dollars of antipoverty programs. These ghetto areas still remain slums. If someone were to drive through North Korea or South Vietnam, they would discover that these nations are still communist, despite the billions of dollars spent to fight the Korean and Vietnam Wars in an effort to destroy communism. In twenty years, it is entirely possible that someone driving through Iraq will find a dictatorship instead of a flourishing democracy. More often than not, governments fail. Few, if any, government programs have accomplished their stated goals. And certainly, no government program ever was shut down because it had succeeded in its mission.

WAR CHALLENGES THE IDEA OF PROPERTY

It is said that the first casualty of war is truth. The second casualty would be property and earnings, or at least the concept that what you earn and what you own belong to you. This is because in times of war, what you own and what you earn are usually confiscated to pay for the war effort.

This is perhaps one of the most overlooked atrocities of governments: the claim that they have a right to whatever citizens own and produce. The reason government can employ this argument is that most citizens are fooled into believing that the state exists to guarantee citizens' assets; that without the state, people would own nothing. In other words, many view government as the protector of private land, lease contracts, and the documents of ownership; all argued to be guaranteed by the state through its police power, printing presses, military force, and insured banking system. Many have been led to believe that without government control and the money to pay for defense, citizens would own nothing because their protector, the state, would no longer exist. But under U.S. Constitutional law, our rights, including private property and the right to keep our earnings, are unalienable. These rights cannot be granted by the state, but belong upon birth to all sovereign individuals. Rights do not come from governments or their agencies. Governments behave like half–crazed wolves on the hunt. They are far more interested in protecting their own political power than in protecting citizens' human rights. In a nutshell, it is people who protect governments; governments do not protect people. By their nature, governing systems must refute the concept of absolute self–ownership and the human right to control one's own labor. The state is in the very business of confiscating property and encouraging a conflict–ridden society.

Yet, how often is it echoed that without the government's right to confiscate citizens' assets and bodies for military affairs, society would collapse into disorder? Ironically, this is the same argument used to support entitlements such as Social Security and Medicare. Whether the confiscation is for military purposes or social purposes, many have come to accept the notion that without forced taxation and controls, women will go hungry, children will die in the gutters, and the old will become homeless—which, of course, did not happen prior to the Great Society that federalized welfare programs in the mid–1960's.

But what might happen during times of economic downturn? Both liberals and conservatives have argued that if economic conditions sour, violent revolution could overrun the ruling government. Some say that to prevent this scenario, government must redistribute wealth in order to preserve order, stave off poverty, and save society. In other words, it is touted that society would not exist if not for the power of the state to tax. The military uses this same argument: forced confiscation is necessary, or society will perish under invasion by one foreign mad dog or another. The welfare/warfare state must control its citizens for the sake of imposing predetermined ideals that are thought to protect all citizens.

What about national defense in times of potential war? Can a country defend itself if it is based on principles of an aggression–free society? Yes. The Swiss had no standing army when the Nazi war machine ground to a halt at its borders in 1940, waiting for Hitler to order a massive invasion. After the German military strategists warned Hitler that an invasion of Switzerland would result in 500,000 German casualties, Hitler's army was ordered instead to invade France, which had a larger standing army and greater numbers of tanks than Germany, but the French citizens were unarmed. The German strategists realized that an armed citizenry in a free nation would viciously fight from every house, every wall, and every cluster of trees. To invade a free, armed society would turn into a guerrilla–style nightmare. As witnessed by the Americans in Vietnam and the Russians in Afghanistan, this type of fighting is deadly to foreign invaders who would rather seize a nation of unarmed citizens and install a puppet regime. Military historians understand that it is almost impossible to defeat a citizenry determined to remain free.

WAR IS ABOUT IMPOSING OUR WILL ON OTHERS

In the case of American interventionism, most wars, including those in Vietnam and Iraq, carry a hidden agenda of wanting to impose our will on other cultures. Wars are often fought to recast strange foreign cultures into something more palatable to the invading outsiders. Unfortunately, the West tends to treat every foreign culture as backward, as if it were a social illness requiring a dose of international co–dependence. Invaders tend to see their own values as virtuous, and believe that the only solution to improve other nations is to have them emulate the so–called superior nation. Certainly, the West has developed a host of technological advantages and democracy, partially due to its system of personal and economic freedom. Yet simply to impose these concepts upon other cultures triggers their instinctive resistance. In other words, neither freedom nor any other concept can be imposed upon others by outsiders.

Just before the demise of the Soviet Union, Russians were moving toward greater understanding of cultural and economic freedom. It had little to do with American military might directed at the Soviet Union. Instead, it had to do with American cultural factors—the proliferation of American lifestyle images, rock music, and bootlegged books and taped TV shows that circulated throughout that country. The average Russian soon discovered how comfortably Americans lived under a market–based system which allowed for greater individuality. They saw the value of individual initiative and freedom. They knew that socialism had failed in every way possible. The Soviet Union collapsed because its citizens finally understood that communism was fatally flawed, and that it could neither feed nor house them as promised. This is in sharp contrast to war. No matter how much someone may agree with something, or how much good it is supposed to produce, forcing it down someone's throat can only instill resistance and conflict.

Mark Selzer is the producer and host of "Libertarian Alternative," a Hollywood-based public-access TV show that interviews authors, activists and leaders in the libertarian movement.   He was the Southern California Vice Chair of the Libertarian Party of California from 2001 to 2007. This article was written in 2007.

CHAPTER 24

THE LIBERTARIAN PHILOSOPHY AND TAXATION

By L.K. Samuels

A government with the policy to rob Peter to pay Paul can be assured of the support of Paul.

-George Bernard Shaw

Why is that quote so amusing? Because we all have seen what a welfare state can do to a society. We know that heavy taxes and spending will not only bankrupt society, but destroy individual liberty. It is the libertarian who has taken the strongest positions in fighting Big Brother and against "government–creep."

Tyranny and taxation are synonymous. Our founders understood this and fought a war over it. Many of them saw liberty as the absence of government control and taxation. In fact, they hated taxation so much that they refused to give the Continental Congress any power to tax American citizens. You've heard countless jokes about George Washington sleeping here and there—well, they're true. Washington traveled a lot because he had to raise funds for his Continental Army. He had no other choice.

So, it should be no surprise that the libertarian philosophy is closely associated with the intellectual father of the American Revolution: John Locke. Back in the 1600's, Locke was one of the first authors to question the authority of government. He said that governments got their authority by permission from citizens, not by the accident of birth. Unelected kings and leaders had no place in his world. But Locke took it one step further. In his Second Treatise on Government, Locke also questioned whether anybody could rule over another unless personal consent was given. In essence, he was not only attacking undemocratic governments, but the validity of taxation without individual consent.

Libertarians believe that government is supposed to serve, not rule; that government should be very limited; and that it should be concerned mostly with protecting individual rights. Through the U.S. Constitution, government was established as a referee, not a player. But we all know that this has failed.

The early libertarians knew that government was the biggest obstacle to prosperity, liberty, and justice. They knew that government was the fox in the henhouse, and that the government which governed least, governed best.

Many of you might feel this is exactly what most of the founding fathers would have said. And you would be correct. Libertarians are the heirs to the classical liberals of the American Revolution—the same people who argued for free markets, individual rights, and minuscule taxes.

Take Thomas Jefferson, for example. He not only questioned government's authority, but the very legitimacy of taxation. He wrote: "To compel a man to furnish contributions of money for the propagation of opinions which he disbelieves and abhors, is sinful and tyrannical." This statement is often attributed to his desire to separate church from state, but also shows his objections to taxation. When Jefferson was campaigning for U.S. President, his main campaign promise was to rid the land of all taxation on U.S. citizens. He kept his promise—the American government ran without taxing its citizens until the Civil War era. If you count the period of the Continental Congress and Articles of Confederation, when the federal government was forbidden to tax at all, America ran for almost 80 years without any direct federal taxes on its citizens. Yet without these taxes, Jefferson's administration was able to retire the Revolutionary War debt—something that even federalists under John Adams and George Washington had failed to do for the previous 12 years.

To understand why taxation is so onerous to libertarians, I will go over the three major pillars of libertarianism: self–ownership, the non–aggression principle, and free choice.

SELF-OWNERSHIP

First, self–ownership. To emphasize this point, I often refer to one of my favorite slogans: "Don't commit suicide; it is illegal to destroy government property." Why is this funny? Because we normally don't think of ourselves as government property. After all, the people and the states created the United States government—a government which is supposed to represent us. However, we all know that government today treats us like property.

The concept of self–ownership can be credited to John Locke. He touched on the idea that each person owned himself. However, this idea did not gain widespread acceptance until the Abolitionist movement started.

In the early 1800's, most people, both in the North and the South, supported slavery. Only the abolitionists and Jeffersonians opposed the enslavement of blacks, and started to refer to it as "man–stealing." The concept of self–ownership was an important milestone. The pro–slavery faction said that blacks were incapable of governing themselves, that they needed to be forced onto plantations so that others could look after them. Sort of sounds like socialism, doesn't it? To counter this reasoning, the early libertarians had to find a strong argument to free the slaves. One of the early abolitionists, William Lloyd Garrison, adopted the principles of self–ownership, and applied it to everyone, no matter where they were from, or the color of their skin.

Ironically, self–ownership was not applied to taxation; before the Civil War, the federal government did not tax U.S. citizens.

Modern libertarians dusted off the concept and made it into a logical axiom which so far, nobody has disproved. It goes like this:

1. I own myself.
2. Because I own myself, I also own what I legally produce.
3. Therefore, nobody can take what I've legally produced, without my permission.

Seems simple. Nobody has the right to take away anybody's wealth without their express consent. But consider
the consequences. This means that the government has no
right to take your hard–earned dollars; that would be theft.
Either we are slaves to the taxman, or we are free. To the
libertarian, there is no middle ground. Jefferson understood
this. That's why he found other ways to finance the federal
government.

Further, backing self–ownership is the Constitution's
thirteenth amendment, which was ratified in 1865 to end
slavery. It explicitly prohibits "involuntary servitude." Under
section 1, it states:

"Neither slavery nor involuntary servitude, except as a
punishment for crime whereof the party shall have been
duly convicted, shall exist within the United States, or any
place subject to their jurisdiction."

So, according to our own laws, we cannot be forced to
serve others. Then again, the government often breaks its
own laws.

But don't we need taxes to pay for all of the wonderful
services the government provides? Libertarians say that if
the government provides worthwhile services, most people
will gladly pay for them. In a free society, people must be
given the choice to pay or not pay. This is what freedom is
all about.

Now some of you might say, "Sure, freedom is good, but
what if the majority supports a particular tax? Shouldn't
the majority rule?" Libertarians say: what about individual
rights? The question boils down to this: how many robbers
must there be before robbery is no longer a crime? How
many rapists must there be before it is no longer rape? We
all know logic. A crime is a crime, no matter how many
people are involved. If the majority of a town goes out and
lynches someone, it is still murder. Majority rule often leads
to mob rule, which tramples on individual rights and self–
ownership.

A good example is the Jim Crow laws in the South. We all know that the white majority had no right to impose their will on the black minority.

THE NON-AGGRESSION PRINCIPLE

The second major cornerstone of libertarianism is the most important one: the non–aggression principle. It says that nobody may initiate or threaten physical force against another. Of course, force may be used in self–defense. If someone swings a knife at you, you have the option to fight back.

It does not matter who initiates the aggression. It does not matter whether a robbery is committed by the Bloods, Crips, Mafia, or the Internal Revenue Service. Theft is theft. This is the whole concept behind individual rights. No matter how many people vote to take away your property, as a sovereign individual, you have the right to keep it. As James Bovard quipped, "Democracy must be something more than two wolves and a sheep voting on what to have for dinner."

FREE CHOICE

The third ideal is free choice. If anything inspirits liberty, it is the concept that each individual has the right to make his or her own choices—a sort of self–governing doctrine. Libertarians argue that individuals know better how to run their own lives than do either a bureaucrat 3,000 miles away or their next door neighbor. In fact, a number of scholars now refer to libertarianism as an "anti–ideology ideology." What does that mean? It means that libertarians do not have a particular pet project to re–engineer mankind in our own image. We can barely run our own lives, and have no intention of telling others how to run theirs.

But more importantly, we do not want to use government force to bring about an "equality of outcome."

Equality of outcome is the socialist tool for making everyone equal. Socialists want to redistribute wealth forcibly, through taxation, to accomplish their concept of utopia. And they have no qualms about using the barrel of a gun to do this. Very Marxist.

From the point of view of physics, nothing is equal. Not even two water molecules on the subatomic level are exactly the same. But most government programs are based on creating equality where none can exist. Winston Churchill understood this, and wrote, "The inherent vice of capitalism is the unequal sharing of the blessings. The inherent blessing of socialism is the equal sharing of misery."

The point to remember here is that nobody should force another to live according to someone else's rules. Sure, people should not eat fatty foods, and should exercise regularly. Sure, we should all donate to charity from time to time. These virtues are choice–driven. But when we force peaceful people to behave a certain way, we are arrogantly saying, "I'm right and you are wrong. And because I am right, you must do as I say, or you will be imprisoned."

This kind of thinking will lead you down the Machiavellian road. Remember Machiavelli? He argued that a noble end justifies violent means. All you have to do is come up with a great idea to change society, and you can use any means to accomplish your program—murder, robber, mass execution. Libertarians say that the ends never justify the means. Period.

Unfortunately, during the twentieth century, the predominant ideologies were various forms of tyranny, social engineering, and authoritarianism. The communists wanted to create the "soviet man"—*homo sovieticus*—who would be completely altruistic and think first of the well-being of others. They sent millions to re–education camps and gulags to cleanse them of their greed and selfishness. The National Socialists under Hitler attempted to create the racial "superhuman" of strength and intelligence. We all know what hideous means they used to accomplish this end. Both of these ideologies had a preordained idea on how man was to behave. Tens of millions died in the name of these so–called noble intentions.

Libertarians like to think of themselves as practical. They know that the best way to bring out the best in man is to allow him the freedom to do what he wants, providing he physically harms no other. Adam Smith realized this. He knew that when people helped themselves in a free market, his "invisible hand" would help the whole community.

Actually, what libertarians say is both timeless and universal. Listen to what Lao Tsu wrote in 600 B.C. in China:

> *Why are the people starving? Because the rulers eat up the money in taxes.... Why are the people rebellious? Because the rulers interfere too much....*

*Why do people think so little of death? Because the
rulers demand too much of life....*

As Chief Justice of the Supreme Court, John Marshall
said, "The power to tax is the power to destroy."
Libertarians are on the forefront to stop this destruction.
We are here to bring liberty back to America. We are here to
create a truly aggression–free society.

Here are a few other good quotations on taxation:

"The only difference between death and taxes is that
death doesn't get worse every time Congress meets."
–Will Rogers, American humorist

"The fact is that government, like a highwayman, says to
a man: 'Your money or your life.'"
–Lysander Spooner, philosopher and abolitionist

"Collecting more taxes than is absolutely necessary is
legalized robbery."
–Calvin Coolidge, U.S. President

This essay was originally presented as a speech to the Marina Rotary Club
in California on August 24, 2005. The manager and co–manager of the
Future of Freedom Conference series for five years in the 1980's, L.K.
Samuels is a writer and libertarian activist. He founded Society for
Libertarian Life (SLL) at the California State University, Fullerton in the
early 1970's. He was instrumental in forming Rampart Institute, based on
the works of Robert LeFevre. Former Northern Vice Chair of the Libertarian
Party of California (2003-2007), he has authored a series of fiction and
nonfiction books, including In *Defense of Chaos: The Chaology of Politics,
Economics and Human Action.* His website is located at
www.Freedom1776.com.

CHAPTER 25

WHO IS "WE"?

By David R. Henderson

One of the beliefs that most distinguished the fascists, Nazis, and communists of the twentieth century was their organic view of society. Proponents of all three ideologies thought of society as an organism—and of each of you, dear readers, as simply a cell in some part of the organism. And just as our cells have no importance outside their ability to serve our whole body, in the aforementioned three ideologies, our whole beings had no importance aside from their ability to serve the whole society. So, of what value was the individual? He was simply a tool for the ends of others, none of whom had importance either, because they, also, were tools. And if society was an organism, then it made sense for the head to run things, right? Government was thought to be the head. And, of course, because there were many people within government, the true head was leader of the government—Mussolini, Hitler, and Lenin or Stalin.

Why is all this relevant to an article by "The Wartime Economist?" Because the organic view of society, though hostile to the basic principles of individual rights on which the United States of America were founded (I use "were" on purpose; "states" is plural) has crept into our language and has distorted much thinking on the issues of the day, including war. It is particularly important in discussions of war, because people are more likely to fall into the trap of seeing war as a conflict between two organisms rather than what it is: a conflict between two governments that, in most cases, have dragooned their countries' resources, with little or no consent from their citizens. So, for example, most people who discuss U.S. foreign policy, including, distressingly, most libertarians, talk about what "we" did when it was, in fact, not you or I, but specific government officials, who took the actions they're describing. They say, "We dropped the bomb on Hiroshima," not, "Harry Truman decided to send a small number of people in the military to drop a bomb on Hiroshima." They say, "The Japanese [or, more commonly, "the Japs"] bombed Pearl Harbor," rather than, "The Japanese government decided to send hundreds of pilots in airplanes to bomb Pearl Harbor." *Et cetera.*

George Orwell wrote a famous essay, "Politics and the English Language," and a famous novel, 1984, making the point that language really does affect thinking. In 1984, he focused on the fact that without certain words, certain thoughts could not be expressed—thus the importance of the government's "memory hole," down which certain words went. In his "Politics" essay, Orwell also pointed out the other side: using words can affect how we think. That is my point here. Specifically, if we use the word "we" to refer to what specific governments have done, and will do in the future, we are adopting the organic view of society, which most definitely will affect how we think.

I saw this in a conversation my wife and I had recently with a well–traveled man we met while in San Antonio. In response to an innocent question about what his favorite place in the world was, he lit into an attack on George W. Bush and Bush's foreign policy. At some points in his rant, he personalized the issue—for example, when he talked about "Bush's war." There's nothing wrong with speaking that way: it is Bush's war. But then he went on to say that the attack of Sept. 11, 2001 was "self–inflicted." It was a predictable result of the U.S. government's meddling in the affairs of other countries, he said. Now, as it happens, I agree with this last statement. But he went on to minimize the loss of 3,000 people on Sept. 11: what did the lives of 3,000 people matter, when millions have been murdered throughout the world? That, I don't agree with. I thought then, and still think, that the loss was horrific and that the people who did it were among the most evil people in history. But that's because I see each of the 3,000–plus people as an individual who matters. He doesn't. Why? Because he has the organic view of society. Go back to his statement that the Sept. 11 attacks were "self–inflicted."

How did the young kid and the 40–something businessman on one of the flights inflict it on themselves? They didn't. So, what did this man really mean? He meant that the U.S. government had helped to bring on the Sept. 11 attacks. But his organic view of society—society as an organism with government as its head—led him to say that the killings were "self–inflicted."

The great tragedy of collectivism, the organic view of society, is that it makes people heartless—they become incapable of seeing the real losses and hurts inflicted on innocent people because they stop seeing them as individuals. The example above is one of someone who couldn't see the hurt that individual innocent Americans suffered in the Sept. 11 attacks. Another example is how hard it is for Americans to see the hurt that the U.S. government inflicts on many foreigners. Two instances come to mind.

While reading a draft of one of my students' thesis chapters a few years ago, I came across the statement, "Fewer than 150 people were killed in the 1991 Gulf war." I wrote in the margin that the number killed was likely in excess of 100,000 people, three orders of magnitude higher than the number he mentioned. When we went over his chapter together, he said that when he wrote "people," he had meant "Americans." His mistake was an innocent one, but it was an innocent consequence of a selective collectivism: seeing Americans as individuals, but people of other societies—particularly ones living in countries on which the U.S. government had made war—as part of an organism.

My second example is like that of the man who thought the attack of Sept. 11 was "self–inflicted." Kevin S., a Navy officer and former colleague of mine at the Naval Postgraduate School, was burned by fuel from the airplane that flew into the Pentagon on Sept. 11. It looked as if he wouldn't live, but he did. It was a heroic story that was written up in his local Virginia newspaper. The article talked about his recovery, and had me cheering for him and his spirit. But then the article stated that Kevin had contacted some of his buddies in the Air Force, and asked them to write on one of the bombs to be dropped on people in Afghanistan, "Kevin sends." As much as I sympathized with Kevin, I was equally sympathetic toward some of the people whom "Kevin's" bomb would injure or kill, who were at least as innocent as he was. Unfortunately, Kevin's collectivist thinking prevented him from distinguishing between those who had hurt him and those who had not.

Collectivism is the ugliest ideology in the world. It has been directly responsible for well over 100 million deaths in the 20th century. Let's do our part by not participating in it, even—maybe especially—in our language. The only hope we have for a peaceful world is to hold guilty people responsible for their actions and to treat the innocent people in all countries as innocent. Let's quit referring to governments whose horrific actions we detest as "we."

David R. Henderson is a research fellow with the Hoover Institution at Stanford University, an economics professor at the Naval Postgraduate School, and the editor of *The Concise Encyclopedia of Economics* (Liberty Fund, 2008). Author of *The Joy of Freedom: An Economist's Odyssey*, Henderson wrote this essay for Antiwar.com on Nov. 3, 2006 in his "Wartime Economist" column.

CHAPTER 26

WHEN DOING GOOD IS BAD

By L.K. Samuels

When the Berkeley Food and Housing Project shut down their "Quarter Meal" program for the poor in 2004, they could hardly believe what had happened. For over 30 years this nonprofit had served dinners to the homeless. They had far-reaching community support, individual donations were up 24% from the prior year, and they had not lost any funding. Still, they had to close their doors. Why?

The city of Berkeley had instituted a new ordinance that required all agencies that received city funding to pay a "living wage." In an ironic twist, the Berkeley Food and Housing Project was one of the prime backers of the ordinance, advocating that all workers get higher wages.

In an example of the "boomerang effect," the mandated wage hike was too much for the food co-op. After raising wages, worker's compensation premiums, and medical benefits, the group discovered over $110,000 in unforeseen expenses. What seems crazy is that after having to close down their program, they still support the ordinance.

This is an example of when doing good can be bad. The city fathers thought that higher wages would help the charity workers. Instead, the workers had to be laid off, while the homeless lost another community-based antipoverty program. The real problem is the fact that government welfare programs pursue good ends by using unsavory means. In other words, government agencies help the unfortunate by hurting the fortunate.

Obviously, it is a good deed to help an orphanage, hospital, or food bank. What could possibly be considered bad about helping noble institutions? Nothing, if doing so is voluntary. Good becomes bad when people are physically forced to provide charity at the point of a gun instead of from the warmth of the heart. Many people assume that if the ends are good, the means do not matter. But do the "ends" really justify the "means"?

That is exactly what Machiavelli advocated in *The Prince*. He believed that government can and should force citizens to do anything, providing that the overall result would be a better society. To take this way of thinking to its logical conclusion, it would permit armed men to force people to work in orphanages, hospitals, and food banks or to do anything else that government deemed good.

Most people want to reserve the right to determine what they do with their time and their lives. But what about the unfortunate and needy? Why can't society forcibly take money from its citizens, or kidnap people or even murder them, in the name of the unfortunate? Why can't we hurt others for the good of all? The problem here is that one person's good deed is another's misdeed. Is this possible? Could anyone justify cold-blooded murder as a good deed? Many serial killers believe that they have helped society in some way. And what about the National Socialists' official policy to exterminate Jews, Gypsies, homosexuals, and others? Most would agree that this was bad, but Hitler and his administration considered it good government policy.

Unfortunately, governments contend in an egocentric way that they are right and everyone else is wrong and that therefore everyone must participate. In truth, a particular governmental program may indeed be important, even helpful. But the good end achieved is not the point. Forcing others to do your bidding is bad. Nobody's pet project is more important than another's life and liberty.

The free meals program in Berkeley would still be in operation if the government had not gotten involved. Unfortunately, the city fathers apparently could not tell good from bad, bringing to mind the old adage, "The road to Hell is paved with good intentions."

This article was published in Nov. of 2005 for the Libertarian Perspective op-ed series, operated by the Libertarian Party of California.

CHAPTER 27

GOVERNMENT-LOVERS AND FASCISM

By L.K. Samuels

In the last few years, President Bush and company have referred to Arab terrorists as "Islamic fascists." The opposition has fired back, arguing that Bush's foreign policy is reminiscent of Hitler's preemptive strikes against Poland and Russia. What has been left out of the political equation is any meaningful description of the term fascism.

Fascism entered the world picture with the rise of Benito Mussolini in the early twentieth century. For years, he had been one of the most famous socialist and labor leaders in Italy. According to David Ramsay Steele (in his article "Mystery of Fascism") "Mussolini was the Che Guevara of his day, a living saint of leftism. Handsome, courageous, charismatic, an erudite Marxist, a riveting speaker and writer, a dedicated class warrior to the core, he was the peerless duce of the Italian Left. He looked like the head of any future Italian socialist government, elected or revolutionary."

But Mussolini had wanted Italy to enter World War I, which caused an infamous split between anti-war socialists and pro-war socialists. This breach in 1914 facilitated Mussolini's break with the Italian Socialist Party and his membership in a radical syndicalist organization called Fasci d'azione Revolutionary International.

When Mussolini became prime minister of Italy in 1922, he began to work more closely with corporations and industrialists. To gain support among all classes of society, he exploited the fear of communist revolution and rival socialist factions. In Mussolini's conception of fascism, the State is the directing force in society, with individuals and all other groups subjugated to it. He poo-pooed democracy and individual freedoms and felt that the vitality of the state depended on its expansion.

President Bush's critics are correct. His policies do resemble Italian Fascism and Hitler's National Socialism (which has also been characterized as fascist), since they impose interventionist foreign policies. But many of those same Bush critics are themselves not free from the taint of fascism. "Contemporary liberalism" in America is rife with highly interventionist economic policies. Many economic policies advocated by the left come directly from Mussolini and Hitler.

For instance, President Franklin Roosevelt plagiarized the concept of Social Security from Hitler's social programs, and FDR's policies that legalized price fixing and oligopoly under the National Recovery Act (NRA) had their roots in Mussolini's cartelization of Italy's economy. The fascist in Italy and German both developed socialized health plans similar to the ones being introduced in the United States today. They were government directed, permitted little individual choice, and were universal except for Jews and undesirables

Italian Fascism and German National Socialism were movements against classical liberalism, laissez-faire capitalism, and free trade. Mussolini sought to amplify the corporate state of the privileged and elite over individual enterprise. He replaced liberal, market-based economics with centralization and government interventionism. Mussolini's formula was notoriously simple: "Everything in the state, nothing against the state, nothing outside the state." By 1939 Italy had nationalized private industry to such a point that it had the highest percentage of state-owned enterprises outside the Soviet Union.

Hitler instituted similar programs, many which are in vogue today. The Nazis called for full employment and a living wage. Using pro-labor rhetoric, they demanded the limitation of profits and the abolition of rents. Hitler expanded credit, opposed the gold standard, instituted government jobs programs and unemployment insurance, protected German industry from foreign competition with high tariffs, nationalized education, imposed strict wage and price controls, and eventually ran huge deficits.

In fact, a number of historians now believe that Germany's economy began to falter in the late 1930s due to its massive armaments build-up, protectionist trade barriers, and social programs. This left Hitler little choice but to roll out his war machine. He had to invade neighboring nations to grab their natural resources and prevent an economic downturn in his own nation.

Today's radical Islamic governments have strong threads of fascism interwoven into their framework. They are nationalistic, rattle their sabers from time to time, and have nationalized large parts of their economies. They have fused government and religion into one big melting pot so that the two are indistinguishable. But this "theofascism" is not only reserved for fanatics hiding among the Islamic faithful. The West has their own religious extremists who are willing to attack non-Christian countries simply because they are "pagan" and therefore evil.

What makes fascism and other authoritarian-based ideologies so dangerous is that they are populated by people who love government. These people bitterly disapprove of the opposition party's policies but are eager to seize the power of government to impose their own particular brand of controls on the populace. Any ideology that puts government before individual sovereignty has all the markings of fascism.

L.K. Samuels is the author of a still-in-progress book, *In Defense of Chaos: the Chaology of Politics, Economics and Human Action.* A Californian Realtor, in 2007 he was elected chair of the Project Area Committee (PAC), a citizens committee to advise the Seaside Redevelopment Agency and the city of Seaside over eminent domain issues. Samuels is winner of the 2007 Karl Bray Memorial Award. This article was written in January of 2007 for *Libertarian Perspective,* an op-ed column promoted by the Libertarian Party of California on a weekly basis.

CHAPTER 28

AMERICA'S TURNING POINT

By Jeffrey Rogers Hummel

The Civil War represents the simultaneous culmination and repudiation of the American Revolution. Four successive ideological surges had previously defined American politics: the radical republican movement that had spearheaded the revolution itself; the subsequent Jeffersonian movement that had arisen in reaction to the Federalist State; the Jacksonian movement that followed the War of 1812; and, at length, the abolitionist movement. Although each was unique, each in its own way was hostile to government power. Each had contributed to the long-term erosion of all forms of coercive authority.

"Nowhere was the American rejection of authority more complete than in the political sphere," writes historian David Donald. "The decline in the powers of the Federal government from the constructive centralism of George Washington's administration to the feeble vacillation of James Buchanan's is so familiar as to require no repetition here. . . . The national government, moreover, was not being weakened in order to bolster state governments, for they too were decreasing in power. . . . By the 1850's the authority of all government in America was at a low point." The United States, already one of the most prosperous and influential countries on the face of the earth, had practically the smallest, weakest State apparatus. The great irony of the Civil War is that it changed all that at the very moment that abolition triumphed. As the last great coercive blight on the American landscape, black chattel slavery, was finally extirpated--a triumph that cannot be overrated--the American polity did an about-face.

Insofar as the war was fought to preserve the Union, it was an explicit rejection of the American Revolution. Both the radical abolitionists and the South's fire-eaters boldly championed different applications of the revolution's purest principles. Whereas the abolitionists were carrying on the assault against human bondage, the fire-eating secessionists embodied the tradition of self-determination and decentralized government. As a legal recourse, the legitimacy of secession was admittedly debatable. Consistent with the Anti-Federalist interpretation of the Constitution that had come to dominate antebellum politics, secession undoubtedly contravened the framers' original intent. But as a revolutionary right, the legitimacy of secession is universal and unconditional. That at least is how the Declaration of Independence reads. "Put simply," agrees William Appleman Williams, "the cause of the Civil War was the refusal of Lincoln and other northerners to honor the revolutionary right of self-determination--the touchstone of the American Revolution."

American nationalists, then and now, automatically assume that the Union's break-up would have been catastrophic. The historian, in particular, "is a camp follower of the successful army," to quote David Donald again, and often treats the nation's current boundaries as etched in stone. But doing so reveals lack of historical imagination. Consider Canada. The United States twice mounted military expeditions to conquer its neighbor, first during the American Revolution and again during the War of 1812. At other times, including after the Civil War, annexation was under consideration, sometimes to the point of private support for insurgencies similar to those that had helped swallow up Florida and Texas. If any of these ventures had succeeded, historians' accounts would read as if the unification of Canada and the United States had been fated, and any other outcome inconceivable. In our world, of course, Canada and the United States have endured as separate sovereignties with hardly any untoward consequences. "Suppose Lincoln did save the American Union, did his success in keeping one strong nation where there might have been two weaker ones really entitle him to a claim to greatness?" asks David M. Potter. "Did it really contribute any constructive values for the modern world?"

The common refrain, voiced by Abraham Lincoln himself, that peaceful secession would have constituted a failure for the great American experiment in liberty, was just plain nonsense. "If Northerners . . . had peaceably allowed the seceders to depart," the conservative London Times correctly replied, "the result might fairly have been quoted as illustrating the advantages of Democracy; but when Republicans put empire above liberty, and resorted to political oppression and war rather than suffer any abatement of national power, it was clear that nature at Washington was precisely the same as nature at St. Petersburg. . . . Democracy broke down, not when the Union ceased to be agreeable to all its constituent States, but when it was upheld, like any other Empire, by force of arms."

"War is the health of the State," proclaimed Randolph Bourne, the young progressive, disillusioned by the Wilson Administration's grotesque excesses during the First World War. Bourne's maxim is true in two respects. During war itself, the government swells in size and power, as it taxes, conscripts, regulates, generates inflation, and suppresses civil liberties. Second, after the war ends there is what economists and historians have identified as a ratchet effect. Postwar retrenchment never returns government to its prewar levels. The State has assumed new functions, taken on new responsibilities, and exercised new prerogatives that continue long after the fighting is over. Both of these phenomena are starkly evident during the Civil War.

Yet the Civil War did something more. Despite wars and their ratchets, governments must sometimes recede in reach, else all would have been groaning under totalitarian regimes long ago. Both conservatives and liberals date the major political turning point in American history at the Great Depression of 1929. Previously Americans are supposed to have self-reliantly resisted the temptations of government largess and confined federal power within strict constitutional limits. Although Franklin D. Roosevelt's New Deal is responsible for Social Security, which now ranks as the national government's primary expense, this legend ignores several inconvenient facts. The New Deal to begin with simply emulated the Wilson Administration's previous war collectivism. Roosevelt's keystone agency, the National Recovery Administration, was a re-creation of the War Industries Board of the First World War; FDR's Agricultural Adjustment Administration was a reactivated wartime Food Administration; the New Deal's National Labor Relations Board trod the path blazed by Wilson's National War Labor Board and War Labor Policies Board; and the Tennessee Valley Authority grew out of the government-owned nitrate and electric-power plants at Muscle Shoals built under the authority of the 1916 National Defense Act. Moreover, the growth of government under the New Deal was trivial compared to its growth during the United States' next major conflict: World War II. Between 1928 and 1938, annual national expenditures slightly more than doubled, from

$3.1 to $6.8 billion. During the Second World War, federal spending peaked at $98.3 billion in 1945. Overall, the national government spent about twice as much while fighting the war as during the preceding 150 years combined. More astute analysts push the watershed in U.S. history back to the Progressive Era. Progressivism emerged at the beginning of the twentieth century as a diverse inclination, varying in different parts of the country and including members of all political parties. But it became the country's first dominant mindset to advocate government intervention over the free market and personal liberty at every level and in every sphere. My contention, however, is that America's decisive transition must be dated even earlier.

The Yankee Leviathan co-opted and transformed abolitionism. It shattered the prewar congruence among anti-slavery, anti-government, and anti-war radicalism. It permanently reversed the implicit constitutional settlement that had made the central and state governments revenue-independent. It acquired for central authority such new functions as subsidizing privileged businesses, managing the currency, providing welfare to veterans, and protecting the nation's "morals"--at the very moment that local and state governments were also expanding. And it set dangerous precedents with respect to taxes, fiat money, conscription, and the suppression of dissent.

These and countless other changes mark the Civil War as America's real turning point. In the years ahead, coercive authority would wax and wane with year-to-year circumstances, but the long-term trend would be unmistakable. Henceforth there would be few major victories of Liberty over Power. In contrast to the whittling away of government that had preceded Fort Sumter, the United States had commenced its halting but inexorable march toward the welfare-warfare State of today.

Jeffrey Rogers Hummel is Associate Professor in the Department of Economics at San Jose State University. He is the author of *Emancipating Slaves, Enslaving Free Men: A History of the American Civil War*. His articles and reviews have appeared in the *Journal of American History*, the *International Philosophical Quarterly*, the *Texas Law Review*, *Econ Journal Watch*, the *Journal of Private Enterprise*, *Independent Review*, and numerous other publications. He has also contributed to the *Encyclopedia of Libertarianism*, as well as such libertarian publication as *Journal of Libertarian Studies*, *Reason*, and *Liberty*.

CHAPTER 29

MORE REGULATIONS NEEDED — BUT ON GOVERNMENT

By L. K. Samuels

The financial meltdown that hit Wall Street and the global financial markets in 2008 was due to the lack of regulations—that is, a lack of regulations on government.

It doesn't take the most competent forensic expert to put the crime scene squarely at the doorstep of the quasi-government banking institutes Fannie Mae and Freddie Mac. These two Government Sponsored Enterprises (GSEs), one of which was founded back during FDR's New Deal, are at the epicenter of the runaway financial meltdown that has enveloped the globe. Without a doubt, they have wielded too much financial political muscle with too little Congressional oversight.

Some political leaders in 2003, mostly Republicans, attempted to rein in Fannie and Freddie, which handle a majority of the $12 trillion mortgage market. The New York Times called these reforms "the most significant regulatory overhaul in the housing finance industry since the savings and loan crisis a decade ago." But the Democrats, especially Rep. Barney Frank, blocked the bill, fearing that it would inhibit loans to low-income households. Calling Fannie and Freddie financially sound just a few years ago, many of the Congressmen opposed to stronger financial regulation were on the receiving end of political contributions by these two state corporations.

In fact, both of these taxpayer-backed corporations together spent nearly $200 million to lobby Congress and financial political action organizations. Much of the money went to affordable housing advocates, political groups, lobbyists, politicians, and anyone who opposed Fannie and

Freddie's excesses. Running wild, these institutions were given all sort of political and financial preferential treatments. For instance, banks are required to retain 10 percent of their capital, but Fannie and Freddie needed to keep only 2.5 percent of their capital, giving them a competitive advantage and the ability to buy even more questionable mortgages. Both corporations are even exempt from SEC filing requirements.

So when did this all start? It appears that the trail of bread crumbs leads back to when President Jimmy Carter helped pass the Community Reinvestment Act in 1977, requiring banks to provide loans to low-income areas, regardless of borrowers' credit worthiness or job history. In short order, banks were successfully sued over charges of racism and redlining when they hesitated to lend to people considered incapable of paying back the loans. Ironically, when banks were reluctant to lend to high-risk borrowers, they were often condemned as racists, yet when they were finally cowed into making loans to unqualified borrowers, many mortgage lenders, including Countrywide, were sued for "predatory lending practices."

Under the lobbying pressure of Fannie and Freddie, Congress was persuaded to mandate these two government chartered corporations to open up the subprime home loan floodgates by the mid-1990s. Subprime loans were now available to anyone with a pulse, regardless of bad credit history and low income. Next, Fannie and Freddie leveraged their advantages, bundling the loans into mortgage-backed securities and selling them around the world. Soon other banks followed suit, determined to remain competitive with the GSEs. Underwriting standards became almost nonexistent in a rush to sell loans to a huge segment of society that could never before qualify for a home loan.

Moreover, another quasi-public agency, Federal Reserve System, had a heavy hand in taking the economy for a harrowing rollercoaster ride. From the outset, the Fed did what it has done so well in the past, especially prior to the Great Depression; it flooded the market with massive amounts of money. In this case, their reckless money machine generated a housing bubble that eventually burst across financial markets and Main Street. The Fed's easy-credit policies had again primed the economic pump with fiat money, which encouraged large and small speculators to get involved in questionable loans and over-priced real estate.

But lowering underwriting standards, disregarding credit history, and promoting "no doc" loans with no down payment were only part of the problem. Another piece of the puzzle involved "moral hazard"—a situation in which people engage in risky behavior because they feel protected. As government-subsidized corporations, Fannie and Freddie would not be permitted to fail. The federal government would always come to their rescue, by cranking up the money-printing press, borrowing, or by increasing taxes. These two government-chartered corporations would never have to bear the full consequences of their actions, since the federal government was always there to bail them out. With such unlimited guarantees, Fannie and Freddie threw open the doors to bad, high-risk loans by privatizing rewards and socializing risk, the essential feature of a mixed economy.

Although some pundits have tried to pin the blame for this mess on laissez faire markets and libertarian ideology, we got into this situation because quasi-government corporations had little fear of financial failure or of greater congressional restraints. Fannie and Freddie got special political treatment and ran recklessly across the political and economic landscape. In essence, the current financial crisis is the result of an unfettered fusion of big business with big government—once known as mercantilism. And when that happens, the out-of-control actions of the corporate state often threaten to sink the ship of state as well as everyone still clinging to the lifeboats.

The 2008 financial meltdown could not have occurred without the interjection of politics into the mortgage industry. A truly free market would have no need of a bailout, nor would it have expected one.

L.K. Samuels is editor and contributing author of *Facets of Liberty: A Libertarian Primer* and a still-in-progress book, *In Defense of Chaos: the Chaology of Politics, Economics and Human Action*. A California realtor, in 2007 he was elected chair of the Project Area Committee (PAC), a citizens committee to advise the Seaside Redevelopment Agency and the city of Seaside over eminent domain issues. Samuels is winner of the 2007 Karl Bray Memorial Award. This article was posted on <u>Lewrockwell.com</u>. Samuels' website is <u>www.Freedom1776.com</u>.

CHAPTER 30

THE ARROGANT SELF-RIGHTEOUSNESS OF VICHY LIBERALISM

By L. K. Samuels

There was a time when liberalism was the undisputed philosophical underpinning of Western Civilization. Consider the first liberal: John Locke's ideals freed the world from kings and tyrants and their arrogant self-righteousness that assumed the citizenry was put on earth just for them to command. The forces of liberalism changed the authoritarian paradigm, leading people to believe that consensus was more important than accidents of births.

But by the 20th century, liberalism had changed, coming full circle. Today the advocates of modern liberalism no longer embrace liberty and tolerance, but a new type of ruler: a benevolent government determined to make people equal by whatever means possible. Government is again the means by which to control society, but this time, for "noble" causes.

Except for the "classical liberals" who still adhered to the traditions of John Locke and Thomas Jefferson, most modern liberals embraced the redistribution of wealth, larger government agencies, and a bureaucratic society dependent on the largesse of the political system. They have legislated womb-to-tomb economic policies reminiscent of 1930s–40s national socialism in Europe, embodied in the Vichy regime in France—hence my term "Vichy liberalism."

Vichy liberals have somehow failed to realize that the larger the ruling authority, the greater the temptation for abuse. In addition, as that abuse enlarges, so does an arrogant self-righteous attitude toward citizens, as if ordin-

ary people were put on the earth merely to provide the
political elite with money and employment.

Illinois Governor Rod Blagojevich's refusal to resign after
being caught trying to sell Obama's vacant U.S. Senate seat
to the highest bidder illustrates this feeling of entitlement.
Saying he had done nothing wrong, the liberal Democrat
also tried to fire some critical editors from the *Chicago
Tribune* and to solicit a bribe from a hospital.

A less publicized case of arrogant disregard for people
occurred in Carmel Valley, California, during the 2008 fires.
Ivan Eberle, a well-known wildlife photographer, was com-
mended for heroism in saving the Monterey Institute for
Research Astronomy observation station on Chews Ridge
from a raging wild fire. A few days after the fire, he was
visited by six Monterey County Sheriffs and charged with
the crimes of battering a firefighter and interfering with a
firefighting crew in the line of duty.

Calling the charges "ironic" and "truly bizarre," Eberle
said he felt that his "constitutional rights were violated to
an egregious degree." To him, the charges filed by the fire
department were in retaliation for his public criticism, as he
had spread the word that the firefighters refused to help
him save the observatory, which is also his home. To
Eberle, the firefighters were acting with "willful negligence
or dereliction of duty."

Eberle believes the bogus charges stem from his quick
actions to save the observatory. When a large tongue of
flames raced toward propane tanks next to a grove of pines,
he unrolled a fire hose from the facility's hydrant and
bumped into a sleep-deprived firefighter. Although the
observatory is the only structure on Chews Ridge, Eberle
single-handedly saved it. Nobody from the fire department
would help. Similar to the theme of Fahrenheit 451, the
firefighters seemed to have forgotten their primary purpose.

So how could such arrogant misconduct occur? Some
have pointed to the consolidation of local volunteer fire
departments with more formal, government-operated ones.
Years earlier in 2001, the Valley Volunteers Inc. in Carmel
Valley Village merged with a government fire department in
the Mid-Valley area. The merger quickly turned sour. In
2004, the volunteer fire department circulated a petition for
"detachment," arguing that their privately-raised million-
dollar fund had been squandered and that the two groups
had different philosophies on how to operate a fire
department. The government agency in charge of such

disputes (LAFCO) refused to allow the separation, although they had earlier said that a "detachment" could easily be arranged if either side found the merger unsatisfactory. Many of the citizen firefighters quit the department, saying that they were being "treated as subordinates" by the new consolidated fire department.

The most dangerous threat from Vichy liberals is that they do not trust ordinary people to do the right thing. Instead, government control and bureaucracy are substituted to run society. Politics and officiality over-shadow anything that citizens attempt to do, preventing society from self-organizing into a system to which people are willing to dedicate valuable time and money. Unfortunately, as consolidation grows, so does an attitude that only government can solve problems, leaving the citizenry defenseless and dependant. Obviously, government has gotten too big for its britches, and its arrogance is showing through.

L.K. Samuels is editor and contributing author of *Facets of Liberty: A Libertarian Primer* and a forthcoming book, *In Defense of Chaos: the Chaology of Politics, Economics and Human Action.* He was recently elected chair of the Project Area Committee (PAC), a citizens committee to advise the Seaside Redevelopment Agency and the city of Seaside over eminent domain issues. He is on the Executive Committee of the Libertarian Party of California. He is winner of the 2007 Karl Bray Memorial Award. His website is at www.Freedom1776.com.

CHAPTER 31

THE LIBERTAS STATEMENT

We, as libertarians, affirm:

That full individual liberty is impossible in any society other than a voluntary one that aggresses upon no one;

That men and women require the full and independent use of their own judgment in order to survive at an optimal level, and therefore have a natural right to do their own thing, providing that they do not physically harm or coercively restrict another individual's life, liberty or property;

That everyone is exclusively sovereign, and is a slave to no one.

That the individual is best served by society when he or she is free from the forcefully imposed controls of others acting alone or in concert (as a government);

That all forms of coercion, aggression and fraud are always immoral;

That the only system consistent with personal freedoms in the economic arena is one that does not interfere with free trade between consenting individuals.

THEREFORE, we, as libertarians, resolve to oppose all forms of aggression by any state, government, self-appointed savior, individual, or association of individuals. We further resolve to oppose taxation, conscription, eminent domain, laws which create victimless "crimes," and all programs forced onto individuals without their consent. It is time that the chains of authoritarianism in economics and morality be broken. Individual rights and coercion cannot co-exist. Liberty cannot be compromised and we will settle for no less than *freedom in our time.*

Adopted on May 5, 1973.

The original "Libertas Statement" was written in 1973 by Society for Libertarian Life (SLL) at California State University, Fullerton.